Military Wives in Arizona Territory

A History of Women Who Shaped the Frontier

Jan Cleere

TWODOT®

GUILFORD, CONNECTICUT
HELENA, MONTANA

A · TWODOT® · BOOK

An imprint of Rowman & Littlefield
4501 Forbes Blvd., Ste. 200
Lanham, MD 20706
www.rowman.com

Distributed by NATIONAL BOOK NETWORK

British Library Cataloguing in Publication Information available

Library of Congress Cataloging-in-Publication Data available

ISBN 978-1-4930-5294-3 (paper : alk. paper)
ISBN 978-1-4930-5295-0 (electronic)

∞™ The paper used in this publication meets the minimum requirements of American National Standard for Information Sciences—Permanence of Paper for Printed Library Materials, ANSI/NISO Z39.48-1992.

This book is dedicated to the women who courageously came with their military husbands into the loosely woven, uncharted land of Arizona Territory.

C. S. Denton

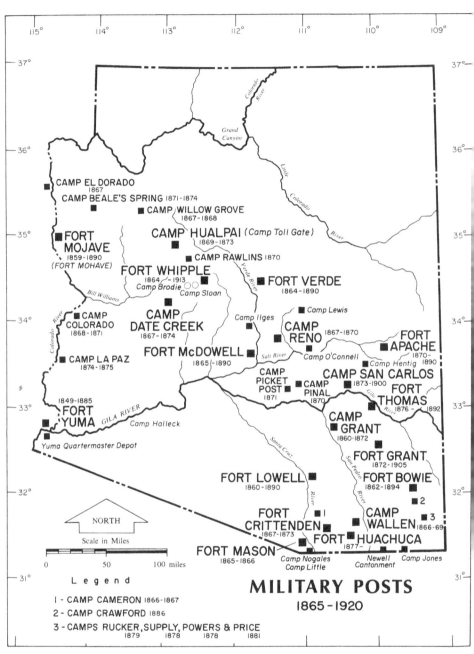

CAMP EL DORADO 1867
CAMP BEALE'S SPRING 1871-1874
■ CAMP WILLOW GROVE 1867-1868
FORT MOJAVE
1859-1890
(FORT MOHAVE)
CAMP HUALPAI (Camp Toll Gate) 1869-1873
CAMP RAWLINS 1870
FORT WHIPPLE
1864 /- 1913
Camp Brodie ○○ Camp Sloan
Bill Williams
FORT VERDE
1864-1890
Camp Lewis
CAMP COLORADO 1868-1871
CAMP DATE CREEK 1867-1874
Camp Ilges
CAMP RENO 1867-1870
FORT APACHE 1870-
CAMP LA PAZ 1874-1875
FORT McDOWELL 1865-1890
Salt River
Camp O'Connell
Camp Hentig 1890
CAMP PICKET POST 1871
CAMP PINAL 1870
CAMP SAN CARLOS 1873-1900
FORT THOMAS 1876 - 1892
1849-1885
FORT YUMA
GILA RIVER
Camp Halleck
CAMP GRANT 1860-1872
Yuma Quartermaster Depot
FORT GRANT 1872-1905
FORT LOWELL 1860-1890
FORT BOWIE 1862-1894
■ 2
NORTH
Scale in Miles
FORT CRITTENDEN 1867-1873
■ 1
CAMP WALLEN 1866-69
■ 3
0   50   100 miles
FORT MASON 1865-1866
Camp Nogales
Camp Little
FORT HUACHUCA 1877-
Newell Cantonment
Camp Jones

MILITARY POSTS
1865-1920

Legend
1 - CAMP CAMERON 1866-1867
2 - CAMP CRAWFORD 1886
3 - CAMPS RUCKER, SUPPLY, POWERS & PRICE
1879   1878   1878   1881

Arizona Military Posts 1865–1920 Walker, Henry P. and Don Bufkin. *Historical Atlas of Arizona.* 2nd edition. Norman: University of Oklahoma Press, 1979, 1986. © 2016 University of Oklahoma Press

CONTENTS

———•●•———

ACKNOWLEDGMENTS

———•●•———

Without the assistance of many individuals around the country who gave of their time to delve into old records, dusty manuscripts, and crumbling newspapers, I would not have been able to present the stories of this handful of amazing women who followed the bugle calls of the Army across the Arizona frontier.

One of my most satisfying discoveries was the journal of Alice Dryer that I found on file at the United States Military Academy. Manuscripts Curator Susan Lintelmann, in the process of moving historic records to a new facility, took the time to search for the journal and provide me with a copy. Without this document, Alice's story would remain untold.

I then went on the hunt for a photograph of Alice. Trying to find pictures of these early women proved daunting, but Brian S. Jaeschke, Registrar of Collections and Archives at the Mackinaw (Michigan) State Historic Park, came up with a handsome picture of Alice.

I had the privilege of interviewing relatives of Army wife Katharine Cochran. Suzy Bradley, Katharine's great-great granddaughter, and Julie Kettleman, great-great-great granddaughter, helped me sort out the identity of the Cochran children and provided me with a photograph of Katharine.

State genealogy organizations came to my rescue on more than one occasion. Mary Carabin, Corresponding Secretary and Researcher of the Huron County Chapter of the Ohio Genealogical Society, provided additional material on the life of Mary Adams, while Patti Seidel and volunteer Mary Lou at the Blair County (Pennsylvania) Genealogy Society spent several hours searching for newspaper articles written by Mary Banks Stacey.

Mary C. Ryan, Editor, Office of the Chief of Staff, Communications Marketing Division (SC), National Archives and Records Administration, graciously sent me a complimentary copy of thè 1981 issue of *Prologue* that I needed for my chapter on enlisted men's wives.

As mentioned, old photographs are sometimes difficult to obtain. With the assistance of the Southern Oregon Historical Society, I was able to acquire a picture of Alice Applegate Sargent.

I visited forts across Arizona, obtaining valuable information wherever I traveled. The Arizona Historical Society is a treasure trove of materials on military personnel who came into the territory even if for a short while. I not only benefited from their written records but obtained many of the photographs in the book from their resources.

I acknowledge the expertise of TwoDot editor Erin Turner, who guided me through several earlier manuscripts and provided a steadying hand when I most needed a kind word. My deepest gratitude for accepting my written words and making me feel like an author.

Of the friends who willingly gave of their time, knowledge, and skill, I want to particularly recognize Arizona military specialist and historian John Langellier for allowing me to ask endless questions about Arizona forts, and Barbara Marriott, who encouraged me to keep looking for those elusive journals and letters as well as reading through my first rough drafts of the manuscript. To my husband, Bob, and my children, your unwavering support of my writing is invaluable.

And to the early military wives who ventured into Arizona Territory, who braved the heat and made homes out of hovels, who courageously sent their children back east to further their educations, or sadly buried them on the bleak and unforgiving frontier, who went wherever their husbands were posted, we owe our heartfelt gratitude for forging through those hard times so that those who followed benefited from their bravery and fortitude. You will not be forgotten.

INTRODUCTION: REVEILLE

———•●•———

In the year and a half that Alice Dryer spent at Fort Yuma, it only
rained twice. Julia Davis envisioned mirages as she departed Yuma
in the mid-summer heat to cross the desert for Camp McDowell. Fannie Boyd was only eighteen years old when she left the comforts of her
eastern home to follow her military husband into Arizona Territory,
and Sarah Upham was only nineteen when she faced an angry group of
Apaches with her child's life at stake.

As Katharine Cochran lined up her children against a brick fire-
place to protect them from a barrage of bullets, and Mary Adams fearfully clutched her infant daughter while her wagon train attempted to
outrun raiding Apaches, Ellen Biddle was twirling around the dance
floor at Fort Whipple.

Mary Stacey took full advantage of her traveling years with the Army,
exploring strange new places and expounding on unique foliage she
encountered. At all of the posts that Alice Sargent lived throughout her
thirty-two years as a military wife, she found Southern Arizona's Fort
Huachuca the most delightful despite the heat, sandstorms, Gila monsters, centipedes, and tarantulas.

These women were the wives of Army officers who came into Arizona Territory from the mid- to late 1800s. They recorded accounts of
their time in the Territory as well as posts throughout the West. Other
women, such as Sarah Bowman and Jane Thorpy, left little documen-
tation of their travels with the military. As Army laundresses, they had

scant leisure periods to jot down their memories, plus their lack of education inhibited their writing propensity. Yet their stories are just as compelling as those of officers' wives, although we have to rely on others to tell of their adventures.

The opinions and prejudices of this handful of women who trekked across uncharted lands present compelling, riveting accounts of what early pioneering women endured, the treacherous journeys they undertook, the children they bore and lost, the substandard housing in which they lived, and the fear of Indian attacks that constantly preyed on their consciousness. Their stories were gleaned from writings by and about them, some written while they were in the territory, others penned near the end of their days.

The accounts are offered as they were composed without addressing particular beliefs or ideologies. They express the moralities and biases of the times. The purpose of compiling these recollections is to illustrate what women bore, tolerated, and sometimes rejected under extraordinary circumstances.

Major C. B. McLellan's Camp on Clear Creek, Arizona, en route to Fort Thomas, Arizona (note Army ambulance in foreground) Library of Congress, LC-USZ62-105873

The majority of the narratives were written by the women themselves, in their own words and style, and offer straightforward descriptions of events that took place during time spent on early Arizona Army posts. Some of their stories presented challenges, such as those of Katharine Cochran, who chose to write of her time with the Army using pseudonyms for her family, leading to some interesting but eventually solvable issues thanks to her surviving kin.

However, not everyone composed her individual chronicle. One proud husband wrote a fascinating account lauding his young bride for her bravery during an Indian uprising.

The majority of these women came from well-to-do families in eastern towns and cities, a few from the South. They left homes and loved ones knowing they might never see some of them again. Choosing to accompany their husbands into the wilds of western living, they could have elected to stay behind and wait for the men to return. Most decided to go wherever their spouses were stationed, not wanting to be left behind. Their husbands were an integral part of these women's lives, which is reflected in their narratives. The husband's career also became the wife's profession.

Yet these were not submissive womenfolk. Whether they traveled west willingly or were reluctant partners, most became strong and independent out of necessity. With soldiers gone for days or weeks on patrol, those left behind on military posts had to handle any event or incident that might occur during this time, including managing households and children on their own.

Some loved their travels and welcomed unique surroundings and new opportunities. Others detested every minute they spent in the west, particularly in Arizona's arid regions.

Those who were fortunate enough to be sent to Fort Whipple in central Arizona found the experience more than delightful as dances, or hops, were scheduled almost weekly, amateur theater performances were constantly in production, and there was a social life similar to what one could expect in cultured eastern cities.

The Army usually encouraged these activities as it relieved the boredom of post life, but there were those who found any presence of women on forts a distinct distraction. Former Army officer Duane Merritt Greene wrote in 1880 that "the presence of ladies in the Army is prejudicial to good order and military discipline . . .," even insisting that an officer who brought his wife to a post "is more prone to shirk duty than the unmarried." He proffered that officers' wives and whiskey were the worst influences on any Army post.

Army wife Fannie Boyd protested and argued for better accommodations and conditions for women who accompanied their husbands: "It is notorious that no provision is made for women in the army," she said. "Many indignation meetings were held at which we discussed the matter, and rebelled at being considered mere camp followers. It is a recognized fact that woman's presence—as wife—alone prevents demoralization, and army officers are always encouraged to marry for that reason."

Housing was particularly frustrating on military posts. Not only were most dwellings subpar, but no sooner did a woman get her house in order, the curtains hung, and the kitchen to her liking than a higher-ranking officer arrived at the encampment and "pulled rank," ousting the woman and her family from a comfortable home to meaner accommodations. This was the norm on Army posts and more than one woman complained of her plight. When Fannie Boyd arrived in Prescott, she was allotted one room in a post house, but the worst was yet to come when more officers arrived and Fannie was moved to an abandoned kitchen where she and her infant daughter slept on the floor.

An officer's wife might feel isolated and alone and sometimes mention she was the only woman at an outpost. What she really meant was she was the only officer's wife in the encampment. Enlisted men also traveled with their wives and families, but these women were ostracized by officers' wives. Likewise, single women who served as servants or laundresses and traveled with military units were considered of lower social class. Most officers' wives felt it beneath them to interact with these working women. Consequently, the isolation described by some officers' wives was a result of their own prejudices.

Few diaries or journals exist that include the struggles and troubles endured by enlisted men's wives. Many of these women were poorly educated, some illiterate. To supplement their husbands' meager salaries, especially needed if the couple had children, they became laundresses for the military or servants in officers' homes. Many served as midwives for women who gave birth on the open frontier, some having more experience than post physicians. They were often called upon to help bury the dead.

Because female servants and laundresses have been an integral part of the military since around 1802, a practice adapted from the British Army, the experiences of these women must be included with others who ventured into the western wilderness. They played an essential role in keeping the military running smoothly.

Sarah Bowman followed the military starting in the 1840s when she accompanied General Zachary Taylor on his foray through Texas and Mexico, and she eventually established a boardinghouse near Fort Yuma. She washed the men's pants and shirts and cooked for ravenous soldiers, even when a post was under siege. Referred to as a "hurricane of a woman" due to her size as well as her personality, Sarah acquired several soldier husbands during her stints with the military, but no one took advantage of this stalwart woman.

Another laundress was Jane Thorpy who, like Sarah Bowman, left no written record of her time with the military, yet piecing together bits and pieces of her life offers a glimpse into the daily drudgery she endured as she followed her enlisted husband from one military fort to another, giving birth to six children on posts across the West, burying three of them.

Sarah and Jane's stories personify the lives of many soldiers' wives who were welcomed into the homes of higher-ranking women as maids, cooks, washerwomen, and nannies but shunned if they happened to meet on the parade ground.

* * *

The writings by and about this collection of women are presented as they were penned over one hundred years ago, although I have taken the liberty of separating longer narratives into readable paragraphs. They are spellbinding and exciting, disheartening as well as thoughtful. They are not politically or culturally acceptable in today's social climate, yet by reading about their hardships and heartaches, triumphs and accomplishments, one can visualize and recognize that these women did the best they could under unpredictable and sometimes harrowing conditions.

The accounts presented within these pages represent many more women who came into the territory and left their mark.

PART I

ARIZONA BOUND

The women who accompanied their military husbands across the desert into early Arizona Territory found the land harsh, unforgiving, and barren. Katharine Cochran quickly noticed the differences as she made her way to Fort Apache in 1879: "From the cold, bracing climate of Oregon we found ourselves in a few weeks on the arid deserts of Arizona, breathing and almost stifling in the dust that was thrown into the ambulance by the wind that always seemed to blow in the wrong direction."

Before the railroad made its way across the continental United States, the most common forms of transportation into Arizona were by wagon, horse, or on foot. Women usually traveled by Army ambulance or in a Dougherty wagon that consisted of two seats facing each other, plus a seat for the driver. The canvas sides of the wagon could be rolled up to allow for more air but if a woman desired privacy, she kept the walls down and drew a curtain between her and the driver.

Some women preferred to ride horseback rather than endure bouncing along a nonexistent road filled with ruts and rocks or deep sand into which wagon wheels unerringly sank, tossing the wagon and its occupants from side to side.

The women described tedious days of plowing through drifting sand and searching vainly for the next water hole. They saw visions or mirages of towering majestic castles and rushing rivers, only to discover these enticing scenes existed solely in their imaginations.

The danger of an Indian attack preyed heavily on the women's minds, and a few did witness uprisings. Their descriptions of these encounters are spellbinding.

Most troops coming into Arizona Territory first made their way to California from varying directions before traveling overland to Fort Yuma. The post actually sat on the western side of the Colorado River on California soil but was under the direction of the Department of Arizona. Established in 1850 to protect gold seekers on their way to California, Fort Yuma provided a much-needed respite for military personnel and their families, who had already endured the trek across the desert from the West Coast. As they began their journey into Arizona to defend the multitude of forts that had been established across the arid terrain, they traveled by horseback and wagon. Others boarded boats at the Yuma port that carried them upriver to Ehrenberg, Fort Mohave, and points east.

Fanny Dunbar Corbusier, whose husband Dr. William Henry Corbusier was stationed throughout the West from 1872 until 1888, seemed to enjoy her voyage along Arizona's riverbank aboard the ship *Newbern* in late 1872. "One day we saw a trapper coming down the river in a canoe," she reported. "Captain Mellon [the ship's commander] called and asked him if he had any beavers' tails. He had, so the Captain laid in a supply and the next morning the Chinaman cook served them fried, along with buckwheat cakes; they were delicious and somewhat like pigs' feet, only better."

Many women, such as Army wife Martha Summerhayes, suspected they were leaving the last bastion of society when Yuma disappeared around the riverbend. Martha penned her recollections of desert travel in her 1908 manuscript, *Vanished Arizona*. She spent two months on the road from Fort Yuma to Fort Apache and once she left Yuma she "felt, somehow, as though we were saying good-bye to the world and civilization, and as our boat clattered and tugged away up river with its great wheel astern, I could not help looking back longingly to old Fort Yuma."

Eveline (Evy) Alexander's journey into Arizona Territory in 1868 illustrates the uncertainties many of these women faced. Evy was pregnant as she made her way by ship from New York by way of the Isthmus of Panama to California, and across the desert by stagecoach and Army ambulance. In writing to her mother after she arrived at Fort McDowell that summer she mentioned, "My condition made me so sensitive to the extreme roughness of the road and the jolting of our conveyance that it was a very anxious journey." Fortunately, Evy gave birth to a healthy baby girl after arriving at the post.

That Evy wrote about her pregnancy, even to her mother, was unusual as expectant women rarely mentioned an impending child until the infant had arrived safely. Martha Summerhayes wrote little about her pregnancy until her son was born at Fort Apache in January 1875.

Mothers fretted over their young children on these harrowing crossings although most youngsters thrived on the pristine air and abundance of sunshine as they scampered alongside the family wagon. Children enjoyed discovering the behaviors of strange new animals. They invented games out of whatever was handy such as tossing around an inflated cow bladder that bounced as well as any store-bought ball.

According to American history specialist Kevin Adams, "American expansion into the trans-Mississippi West was not solely a move-ment of peoples, it was also a movement of food, drink, clothing, and furniture—a caravan of consumer goods that reconfigured the region's economy and society. Nowhere was that truer than in the United States Army."

Officers were given an allowance of one thousand pounds of baggage on their treks across the desert; enlisted men were apportioned much less. As soon as orders were received to move out, wives started packing only the necessities they would need to make it to the next post. Large items, such as furniture and bedding, were sold or left behind for the next occupant of their humble abode. And hopefully, residents who had recently departed from the next post also abandoned an array of items that could be used by the new tenants.

* * *

Of the many women who made the journey across the desert into Arizona Territory, only a handful left written records of their adventures. In 1860, Alice Dryer traveled from New York to the West Coast traversing the Isthmus of Panama, a long, tedious voyage for many of those coming from the east. Her trip ended once she arrived and settled at Fort Yuma. Alice did not pen her reminiscences until sometime after 1906 and before 1918, the year she died.

Julia Davis stopped briefly at Fort Yuma in 1869 before going on to Camp McDowell with her infant son. She dictated her narrative shortly before her untimely death in 1873 at the age of twenty-four.

Mary Stacey also tarried at Fort Yuma before going on to Fort Thomas in 1878. She penned lengthy letters to her mother about her travels and adventures. Her mother had Mary's correspondence published in a local eastern newspaper. Mary loved to travel and made the most of her excursions, whether they be by ship, rail, or in an Army ambulance.

All three of these women described the phenomena of mirages they envisioned while traveling across the desert, imaginary fantasies seen by most who trudged their way through deep, challenging sand with temperatures often hovering well above 100 degrees. Fortunately, they knew what they were witnessing and did not succumb to the temptation of chasing after these illusory hallucinations.

If these women knew or had knowledge of each other it is not recorded, but the experiences they encountered on their journeys, as well as the time they spent on Arizona Army posts, may have passed from one woman to another, told and retold to military wives who followed them.

CHAPTER 1

---•••---

Miles and Miles of White Burning, Blinding Sand

Alice Garrison Dryer

In 1860, when Alice Dryer started across the desert from the California coast to Fort Yuma, she may have wondered if she had made a dreadful mistake. The heat, the sand, the persistent swaying and rocking of the wagon, not to mention the constant search for water continued day after day with no relief or respite. She tried to shield herself from the sun's blistering rays, yet her skin turned a bright blistering red and then a golden tan, not at all what a proper eastern woman favored. But she was determined to go wherever her husband was ordered, although the deserts of Arizona were not where she had hoped to land.

Fortunately, Alice's journey ended at Fort Yuma, which was physically in California but under the military Department of Arizona. The

Alice Garrison Dryer circa 1870s
Photo courtesy Mackinac State Historic
Parks Collection

Yuma Depot, on the Arizona side of the Colorado River, housed supplies for camps located in the Territory. Ferries transported provisions
back and forth between the two facilities.

Alice had accompanied her husband, First Lieutenant Hiram Dryer,
on what she thought would be a tour of duty at Fort Vancouver, Washington Territory. Hiram had enlisted in the Army in 1846 during the
Mexican War and distinguished himself throughout his career, rising
within the ranks to the position of major by 1865. He was a first lieutenant when he married Alice Garrison, who claimed Detroit, Michigan,
as her native city.

Probably not a young woman when she married fifty-year-old Hiram
in 1859, Alice went with her husband wherever he was posted throughout his military career. Her descriptions of the often-stark military posts
at which they were stationed were less than laudatory.

The couple started their journey west by sailing out of New York for
the Isthmus of Panama. Hiram might not have been overly enthusiastic
about the trip as this would be his second crossing of the Isthmus to
reach the West Coast. The first time, in 1852, 104 men had died from
cholera on the expedition.

Alice's account of her travels, chronicled in her booklet, *Reminiscences of an Army Woman*, which she penned sometime after her husband died in 1867, reveals a woman used to comfortable surroundings
but who also loved her husband enough to stay with him no matter
where he was ordered to go.

She found the sea voyage down the Atlantic Coast delightful. As
they headed across the Isthmus, however, she became concerned about
"contracting the Panama fever in a hot, damp atmosphere which was
conducive to the ripening and perfecting of the native fruits, especially
bananas and pineapples, even though the air was not good for man . . .
It was a delight to board the elegant Pacific steamship when we reached
the other side of the isthmus. They were such an improvement on the

Atlantic steamers, larger by far, more comfortably furnished, and best of all, kept scrupulously clean.

"The trip from Panama to San Francisco was enjoyable," she continued. "For two weeks we glided along in this floating palace on the peaceful glassy waters of the Pacific—no such thing as seasickness known on that side. We made several ports on the Mexican coast, anchoring out in the harbor in sight of dock, but not landing."

From San Francisco, the party headed to Fort Vancouver, Washington Territory. As soon as they arrived, they were ordered to Los Angeles to begin the difficult and dangerous journey to Fort Yuma.

Back in California, Alice took advantage of a few days' reprieve before the troops headed into Arizona by touring the nearby wine country, a venture that proved advantageous once she started across the desert.

"The native sour wines were used as an ordinary beverage on every table," she noted. "And we took a supply with us which many times in crossing the desert had to be used in place of water. We were nearly three weeks in crossing the desert and sometimes where we camped the water was undrinkable."

Alice was one of the few officers' wives to travel with the troops across the desert this early in the Indian campaigns, struggling through ankle-deep sand, always on the lookout for sources of water. Her description of the crossing echoes that of other women who later accompanied the troops.

The length of the marches across the desert had to be made according to where we could find wood and water—both of which were scarce articles—so the day's journey varied from ten to fifteen miles, longer marches could not be made in the burning sun and heavy sand. As it was during the hottest season of the year we had to make very early starts in the morning. We were awakened by fife and drum sounding reveille as early as 3 a.m.

some mornings, when there was a longer march to be made that day, so that we could be out on the road before sunrise. There was no time to be sleepy or to dally.

The camp fires were going betimes and we soon smelt the coffee and bacon for our breakfast. It is not necessary to say that it was always relished—no such appetite can be gained from the present day tonics as our out of door life gave. All bedding, camp kit, etc., had to be ready for the men to put into the wagons at a certain moment when the call was sounded to strike tents. Oftentimes we commenced our day's journey by moonlight or starlight, and were always in camp by midday. Once we tried a night march instead of by day, but it was not satisfactory, as the soldiers were more pulled down by it than by day marching.

The officers and men led the line, next came the ambulances or carriages with officers' families, then the line of wagons of six mule teams hauling the tents, baggage, etc. The last named had to travel very slowly and late getting into camp with the stuff, for which we could do nothing but patiently wait. We hailed the cloud of dust with delight, as it betokened their approach ever so far off. The four gray mules which drew my ambulance would rarely go off a walk, as the soft sand often reached the hubs of the wheels.

It was monotonous and wearisome for women, but harder for man and beast (the men sometimes gave out and fell down by the roadside and waited for the hospital ambulance to come along and pick them up). Few of the officers' wives undertook the trip, as they could not bear being dragged at snail pace through miles and miles of white burning, blinding sand, day after day for three weeks, Sundays no different from weekdays, to all outward appearance. One can imagine how the weary eye eagerly stretched its gaze ahead to try and catch a glimpse of distant trees, for there we would find a stream of water of some kind and get a little relaxation from our cramped position by sitting or lounging under the shadow of a tree while waiting for the wagon to come in with the tents and camp chests. . . .

There was very little variety in our long march from Los Angeles to our place of destination, Fort Yuma, noted especially for being the hottest place in the world. (Cheerful to look forward to!) The camping places along the road were all dignified with names, as if they were towns, but when we reached them we found only a few trees beside a stream or creek, and a whisky shop wherewith to tempt our soldiers. We generally picked our camping ground as far as we could from the latter snare.

Alice and her party were not immune to desert hallucinations that weary, thirst-driven travelers often envisioned as they gazed into the blazing sun.

We were once entertained by a very beautiful mirage which looked like a large city in the distance, and which we never seemed quite able to reach. The atmospheric illusions were very pleasing for the time being, even though we found the foundation of our picture to be nothing more than a dry alkali lake, which was very white and visible for several miles, giving the impression of a far off city or castle. We also sometimes came across an old mission in the neighborhood of our camp, which was most interesting. These were founded chiefly by the Franciscan Fathers, who were most courteous to us when we met them. But oh! The relief and the delight of seeing our dear Stars and Stripes waving its welcome to weary travellers [sic] as we came in sight of our home [Fort Yuma]; it was home, no matter what discomforts or disadvantages might prove to be.

Alice found little to please her in a post remiss of shade, trees, shrubs, and grass.

"[N]othing green visible to the naked eye," she complained, "nothing but bare rock and sand reflecting the heat like a fiery furnace."

She did marvel at the gardens that nearby Native and Mexican families cultivated close to the riverbank, and admired the rows of lettuce and succulent peppers that thrived in the searing heat. But she distressed over not being able to keep butter as it almost immediately melted into oil.

"The water was put in oyers [ollas or clay pots]," she said, "made by the squaws, which were suspended in the air on the piazzas, wrapped in gunny sack or blankets kept wet. This process kept the water cool—or at least what we call cool in that country."

Post housing also left her less than satisfied:

> *The quarters were built of adobe and three feet thick, they did not keep the heat out, for the walls were so hot on the inside that you could scarcely bear your hand on them during the summer. . . . Beds and mattresses were deserted; one could only sleep on canvas-covered cots with linen sheets and a hair pillow for bedding, and that outside in the inclosed [sic] piazza—cots had to be carefully screened from mosquitoes, as they were not of the ordinary kind but very large and very fierce, leaving a stream of blood trickling down from their bite. . . .*
>
> *Soldiers went on guard in their shirt sleeves and had to wear Panama hats with a wet cloth inside to protect them from the intense heat and liable sunstroke. Not a very military sight, and even they succumbed to the sun's rays and averaged two and three deaths a week from sunstroke during the hottest weather. The hospital being opposite our quarters, we could distinctly hear the groans of the sick and dying. The dead*

march became a mournfully familiar sound on the fife and drum as they carried these poor men to their last resting place in the cemetery below the fort.

The wives of the officers, the sutler, the postmaster and the steamboat captain, who lived over the river, all left the country before the very hot weather began. Afterwards it would be too hot to cross the desert. I chose to stay, and consequently was the only white woman there except the camp laundresses who had to stay and work. I could not be persuaded to leave my husband to bear alone the discomforts of this forlorn country, and as it was my first post I felt it would be cowardly to desert him for my own personal comfort.

In October and November the temperature began to drop a little, so that after sunset we could walk out or ride on horseback down to Pilot Knob [a volcanic landform that was used as a landmark by riverboat pilots], which was about all the recreation we had. The arrival of the overland mail once or twice a month was a great event—sometimes six weeks would pass without our hearing a word from the states, owing to the stages being attacked by Indians or because of bad roads. It was one of our few pleasures when we got the mail to meet and exchange the news one with another. This post was established to protect the overland mail, as the Indians in that part of the country were very troublesome at that time. [Fort Yuma was a stop for the Butterfield Stage from 1858 until 1861.].

Our commissary stores and supplies were brought from San Francisco to Fort Yuma by water down the coast and up the Gulf of California, but the one thing we craved and needed—ice— could not bear transportation.

Occasionally during the winter a wagon would arrive from Los Angeles with grapes which were a great treat.

We had rain only twice during the year and a half of my stay there, and that, instead of cooling the air, rather had the effect of a vapor bath, which necessitated the immediate change of clothing. The Indian women there wore only one garment, that being made into a skirt of strips of willow fastened into a belt at the waist and reaching to the knees—little bells attached to the strips so that their approach was heard fortunately. Scorpions and centipedes abounded in this country, as well as armies of formidable ants which moved in upon us in large bodies at intervals.

The stir in this region was only cooled by sandstorms, which were an occasional relief; when they came everything had to be put away and covered closely, as the fine sand penetrated books, clothing and every exposed article in the house.

When the Civil War heated up in the East, Hiram's unit was called back to the States. "As it was in the cool season," Alice wrote, "we crossed the country very comfortably to San Diego. One feature of this march was the Temecula canyon [California], through which we had to pass—so very rough with rocks and steep in places that a rope had to be wound around my ambulance many times to keep me in."

Safely back on the West Coast, Alice waited for a steamer that would take her from San Francisco to Panama. She joined several other Army wives who were also on their way east to a different type of war than what they had experienced in the West. Alice learned her tour of duty, although difficult, had not been as harsh as what others endured.

We Army women were glad to meet again and during our long voyage home had ample opportunity to talk over our experiences and compare notes. Some of the ladies I found had been situated more uncomfortably than we at Fort Yuma in some respects. Our heat was more intense, but at Fort Mojave the quarters were wretched, with thatched roofs and houses old and uncomfortable. It rained there more frequently than at Fort Yuma, and leaked through so that they had to sit under umbrellas, and the children got under the tables to keep dry, and many other amusing inconveniences which we were able to laugh over now that we were well out of them.

One of Alice's many disappointments during her western tour of duty was the lack of churches. "In all my year and a half at Fort Yuma," she said, "I never saw a church or a priest, but a church woman can always find comfort in her prayer book and united with the dear ones far away in the church services."

Alice arrived in New York just before Christmas 1861. "We were not allowed to touch dock until the next morning," she said, "but one lady and myself with our husbands got off and went to a hotel in the city, late though it was. We had both suffered in outward appearance by our exile and in our old-fashioned, dilapidated clothing made rather a grotesque and incongruous picture in a fashionable hotel in New York city."

The Metropolitan was the Army hotel of that day. As we were passing a long mirror at the end of the hall on our way to supper we suddenly confronted ourselves, at first not recognizing the forlorn-looking women, but finally, very much amused and not at all disconcerted; we came home like soldiers from battle— rather proud of our scars in the service. We had left home young and fresh only a year and a half before and now our dearest friends did not know us when we reached our native land. Thin and brown, the color of the adobe houses and the Indians, weighing less than 100 pounds, it was no wonder I was not recognized.

Hiram served valiantly during the Civil War, rising in the ranks to major while he was stationed at Camp Dennison near Cincinnati, Ohio. In December 1865, he assumed command of Kansas's Fort Larned, which, according to Alice, was almost as bad as living at Fort Yuma but at the opposing end of the thermostat.

"Very cold weather, dead frozen cattle lying all around outside the fort, and for officers' quarters a row of one story log rooms all connected, lined with canvas, thatched roofs, mother earth for floors, etc." Alice also complained that the recently departed volunteer troops had "stripped the fort and left nothing."

Fortunately, their stay at Fort Larned lasted only until April 1866, when Hiram was ordered to Fort Randall, Dakota Territory.

The following March, the major came down with a severe cold that turned into pneumonia. On March 5, 1867, Hiram Dryer died at the age of fifty-eight. Alice took him back to Detroit to be buried in the family plot.

Sometime around 1906, Alice returned to Los Angeles, California. She noted it had been forty-five years since her last trip west and she found the city unpleasantly transformed.

"The town is no more the little Spanish place that it was when I first saw it, but changed into a large, noisy, bustling American city, with high buildings, packed closely together, thickly populated, a brisk business carried on, people rushing to and fro, jostling one another as they pass, street cars running every direction and last and worst of all, the inevitable automobile which one encounters everywhere these fast days. I was glad to get out of the great noisy city . . . no more vineyards were to be seen near the town."

Alice eventually entered the order of the Community of Saint Mary in Peekskill, New York. Taking the name Sister Alice, she resided there until her death in 1918.

CHAPTER 2

I Resolved to Go!

Julia Edith Kirkham Davis

As she hand-stitched a garment for her five-year-old son, Julia Davis chatted with an old friend about her 1869 adventure crossing the desert from San Diego to Fort Yuma and on to Camp McDowell. Fortunately, the friend recorded the conversation shortly afterward since twenty-four-year-old Julia died just a few days later.

While Julia was often described as delicate and in poor health, the fact she made the arduous desert crossing of her own volition, and lived in desperate housing while at Camp McDowell, attests to the fact she had the strength and endurance to conquer whatever she undertook.

Julia was born sometime between 1848 and 1850 to Ralph and Catherine Kirkham. Her early life was comfortable as her father had experienced an eminent military career, attaining the rank of Brevet Brigadier General. Retiring from the military in 1870, he relocated his family to Oakland, California, and became a successful businessman.

Julia's mother, Kate as she was called, was a founder of Oakland's Fabiola Hospital, which provided medical aid to everyone regardless of their financial situation.

In 1863, Julia attended Oakland Seminary for Young Ladies, considered the first girls' school established west of the Mississippi River. The 1869 curriculum consisted of reading, spelling, geography, arithmetic, history, penmanship, and composition.

On May 5, 1868, Julia married Captain Murray Spurzheim Davis, who was serving as an aide to Major General Henry W. Halleck, commander of the Division of the Pacific at San Francisco. Davis served during the Civil War and had just completed a tour as the first post commander of Camp Winfield Scott, Nevada.

The newlyweds set out immediately for a grand tour of Europe, but not before Murray requested an extension of his leave "for the benefit of my wife's health which is very feeble and I fear she will not be able to return during the present year." His request was granted.

Seven months later, while the couple were in Nice, Alpes-Maritimes, France, Julia gave birth to a son, Stanton. Murray again requested a leave extension because he claimed his newborn child "is now very sick and I fear will have a serious battle for his life. . . .If four months can not be obtained three, two or even one will aid me some," he begged.

Finally arriving in New York in May 1869, Murray petitioned for one more allowance on his leave as he had trouble obtaining his luggage from the custom house and had missed the ship sailing to Panama and on to California. He argued, "The health of my family is such that I can not proceed overland and I propose to sail by the next steamer."

Finally landing in California, Murray immediately received orders to go to Arizona. He settled his wife and son in Oakland and headed to San Diego to rejoin his unit.

How delicate in health were Julia and her son is unrecorded except for her husband's pleas for leave extensions to care for his family. Yet regardless of the frailty of either, Julia was determined to go with her husband and not be left behind.

"My baby was just six months old," she recalled, "and I was, oh such a mere girl to look at, and not nineteen; and everybody said I must stay here and let him go alone. So he thought too, and it was settled so. He fixed me up in a little home here, and left me, alone. All my people were in Europe, and though I had friends in Oakland and San Francisco, I felt dreadfully lonely. I thought of my husband going down and the dangers of Indian warfare, and being perhaps killed by savages, whilst I was far away; and I could not bear it."

I had a letter from San Diego to tell me he [Murray] would begin the march from there on Wednesday the next week. It was then Friday. If I could make arrangements in two days, there was a boat which would carry me to him by the following Tuesday. I resolved to go!

All my friends of course cried out I was mad. I should die of hardship and fatigue, and my husband would have to bury me in the desert. My answer was that I should certainly die if I stayed fretting here alone, and if I was to die, I would rather my husband should bury me than strangers; so I should go.

Well the nurse and I set to work, we fixed up the baby, we packed, we prepared, we arranged. I took linen, books, a bed, pictures, curtains, everything I could think of for housekeeping; for I learnt that when I got to Arizona, I should have just what I took there, and nothing more. I had another reason, too, for carrying a quantity of baggage. I reckoned it would cost so much taking it all down, that it would be impossible for me to come back; and I felt sure enough that to send me back would be my husband's first notion.

With the aid of a kind friend, I made everything ready, we were all fixed in good time; he saw me on board the steamer, and we started, nurse, baby and I for San Diego.

On Tuesday morning we were at anchor, and my husband hurried on board expecting letters from me, and you may fancy his surprise when he found myself. That I was to return by the same boat, was, as I expected his immediate verdict; but that I told him was impossible. All my available funds would not carry me back, and I had everything ready for the journey.

Of course there were plenty of remonstrances, but the force of my arguments was irresistible. I could not go back, I would not stay at San Diego, and the only alternative was to proceed with him. He yielded to necessity and went out to procure a vehicle to carry me. It was of course the regular white topped wagon, with four horses in which I should have to make a six weeks journey over the desert along with my baby and his nurse. [Julia probably traveled in an Army ambulance or Dougherty wagon, a standard form of military transportation at the time. Rarely were covered or Conestoga wagons used by the military.]

A mattress was laid in it, and in this we were to live, sleep and travel, the only change being to the saddle when I chose to ride. Indeed horseback for the first two days was my only resource, for the wagon horses were perfectly wild and unbroken mustangs, and not safe until tamed by work and hardship, so whilst Lulu [the nurse] and baby were packed in a baggage wagon, I rode with my husband.

I had prepared myself for this and dressed accordingly. A blue serge dress, no hoops or extra skirts, my hair braided in one long tail, and a hat on my head nearly large enough to hide me entirely, that was my get up for the journey, and being so small and light, (I only weighed 90 lbs.) I looked quite like a girl.

Well we started from San Diego and were soon sensible that we were going farther and farther from civilization. Our route lay through a desert—oh such a desert—sand, white glaring sand and alkali dust all round us, not a tree, not a shrub, not a green thing of any kind, and the monotony only broken by rocks, frightful hideous rocks here and there, staringly [sic] blankly at us, with nothing to hide their barren ugliness. You cannot fancy such a country!

Every day the sun came up fierce, unclouded into the dazzling sky, and burned over our heads, and grew hotter and hotter, and the alkali sands scorched our eyes, and choked us until we gasped for breath, and the heat from the ground seemed greater even than the heat from the sun.

Thirst—oh one does not know what thirst means until one has toiled on under such a sun, and without water for hours together.

There were very few springs or creeks, from one station to another, generally none where the water was drinkable; and can you fancy what it is to come on a stream beautifully clear and delicious in appearance, and find it so bitter that even the very horses turned from it with disgust.

How the soldiers suffered, poor men. They would start from the station, each with his canteen full, and rolled up in a wet blanket to keep it cool as long as possible, but often long before we reached another supply every drop would be gone, and they had to toil on as they could.

Then the heat grew too great to move by day at all sometimes, and we only marched by night. Those delicious nights. As the sun went down, and the longed for coolness of evening came to refresh us, I would sometimes have the wagon cover removed, and then lying on the mattress slowly travelling on, I watched the stars rise and pass across the sky until they went out in the morning light. Yes, California skies are clear, and the stars here are bright, but they are nothing I think compared with the brilliancy of those desert scenes. There seemed to me thousands more stars visible than I ever saw before, and so intensely vivid, so clear, and yet so far off. . . .

We had an alarm every now and then, but the body of troops was too large for there to be any great danger, so long as ordinary precautions were attended to. We had scouts, and sentinels and were careful to keep a good look out, and no stragglers were allowed. It would not have been safe for even a small party. We knew the Indians were watching us, and we never knew when they might attack.

Maricopa Wells circa 1870 Arizona Historical Society, Places-Maricopa Wells Photo File, #28991

According to the records of the Regimental Returns, Eighth Cavalry, which was Murray's unit, the route took the party from Fort Yuma along the Gila River and on to Maricopa Wells, a stopping off place for travelers coming out of the desert. Friendly Maricopa and Pima people offered sustenance to those who survived the journey from Fort Yuma. From Maricopa Wells, the troops headed north to the Salt River. If Julia thought she had survived the worst of the crossing, she soon learned the desert was not yet through with her.

After passing Fort Yuma we were in the Indian country and had quite left all civilization behind. But though we had no stragglers our line was very long, and the heavy baggage wagons would fall into the rear, so it not infrequently happened that we arrived at the station where we were to halt, whilst they were far behind, and we had to wait hours sometimes before we could get food or anything we needed. That was very weary work.

Then the most tantalizing thing of all was the mirage. I used to see it constantly before us, the most exquisite landscapes, clear lakes, and green islands, and scenes of beauty perfectly heavenly; there in the distance flying before us. I could not believe them false at first, one reads of the mirage, but it is quite another thing to see these heavenly scenes, and be tantalized by such delusions. They made the heat hotter, and the desert drier and the sand more choking than ever.

At length one day my husband told me our journey was drawing to a close, and that next morning would bring us to the camp [McDowell]. That night I could not sleep from excitement, and I was picturing to myself what my future home would be through all the weary miles that intervened.

Then came the exclamation, there it is. This is Camp Mac Dowel [sic], we have reached our destination.

The Davises arrived at Camp McDowell on September 1, 1869, three months after they left San Diego.

"I looked in vain. I could see nothing!" Julia cried. "There were the same scorched mountains, the same uncouth rocks, the same dazzling sand, the same glare, and drought, but where was the camp; the dwellings, the home of which I had been dreaming? Those low mounds which looked only like hillocks, as we drew near; where I discovered the dwellings, and to one of them I was finally conducted as my residence.

"A two-roomed adobe hut, with mud walls, and floor, open to the thatch of brush, and without an article of furniture. This was our refuge, for this I had left civilization and comfort and security!"

Camp McDowell, headquarters for the District of Arizona from May until August 1869, housed over 470 men. It was far from comfortable. Julia's home consisted of an adobe-walled house with a roof constructed of mud and horse manure. These rudimentary rooftops managed to keep out water during Arizona's sporadic rainy spells but when monsoons hit in late summer, a pungent odor permeated the living quarters. Beds were covered with rubber blankets to keep them dry.

"The officers crowded around with amazement to see the newcomers," Julia said, "the lady; of course we two women, my nurse and I were the greatest curiosities. There was already one other lady in the camp, and now the female society would be doubled."

As did most officers' wives, Julia did not consider the enlisted men's wives nor any laundresses as "ladies." She did not even regard her baby's nurse in her same social category, leaving one other officer's wife that she decreed her equal.

Our welcome was the warmest, what ever could be done to make us comfortable was done immediately, but I felt how much depended on myself, and set to work with all my heart.

Thankful I was now for all the baggage I had carried. The bed was put up, the pretty lace curtains arranged both for it and for the window; and I had beautiful linen, part of my wedding out-fit. But tables and chairs were things unknown in the camp, rough boxes and chests served the purpose. There were many ready to assist me but I had to improvise and invent, I had no idea of sitting down on a packing case, and gazing on mud walls, if I could do better. Happy was I when I succeeded in having those mud walls whitened, when I hung up my pictures, arranged my photographs and placed my books on the shelves improvised from a packing-case. Our own trunks and boxes covered with the gaudy chintz which was all I could get at the sutler's store, and with their tops well stuffed with hay, supplied us seats and lounges; of various shapes and sizes it is true, but the more picturesque for that. Packing cases were so valuable, that it was with difficulty I could procure more; but I did coax one old sergeant out of what I needed, though he said he only gave them for my young face. . . .

Packing cases made everything; toilet-table, seats, book case, sofa, wardrobe—all the necessities of life; but you would not have guessed it, chintz and muslin and a little skillful arrangement did wonders.

Coming from a family of wealth, Julia surprisingly took to her new surroundings with enthusiasm and aplomb. "It was the cunningest little house when it was all fixed up," she gushed, "and the wonder of every body who saw it. And before the cold weather, and it is cold there too, I had a chimney contrived and a hearth, and the blacksmith made me a pair of iron dogs and when we had a fire it was just as nice as it could be. I loved that little home dearly, and never repented having gone there."

Julia, however, did complain that Camp McDowell "was no place for gardening, desert, sand and rock, not a green thing to be seen, only a few scrubby mean little manzanita bushes; nothing else could live, and they were half dead; it was no use to cultivate anything. I had dreamt of a tropical vegetation, and forests and prairies. I found as I say, a desert, great bare purple rocks, and still more bare tracks of sand.

"And as to walking, one dared not go half a mile from the camp without an escort. There might at any time be Indians lurking round; and it was not safe. Now and then I did ride out with my husband, but it was risky even with a large escort, and hardly any pleasure."

I Resolved to Go!

The summer before Julia arrived at Camp McDowell, even the mail came by circuitous route through San Francisco because of Indian uprisings:

Oh those dreadful Indians, you know they were always lying in wait, and our party might be cut off, and have to fight, and their arrows are poisoned, so if they do not kill they wound mortally in most cases.

They used to come into camp sometimes to have a pow-wow great parties of them, and we always had to be on our guard then, lest they should break out and attack us suddenly. Horrible great men, all but naked, and painted to look uglier than nature made them with their dreadful sheaves of arrows, and their cruel faces; one never could trust them, and I use to be in agonies of terror when there were many about.

We never were attacked really, though we had more than one alarm: we were too cautious for them.

But the worst was when my husband had to go out scouting, then I confess I was in terror. It seemed to me I should never see him come back, and each time it grew worse; at least my fear did: for every now and then they would bring back wounded men, sometimes they brought dead ones: they never left any to be scalped, but oh it was sad, sad to see the poor fellows coming back to die slowly and painfully, so far away from home.

I knew most of my husband's men, and could visit and try to comfort them, but there was little to be done, except by kind words; we had no comforts for sick, no fresh meat, no milk or eggs; only canned provisions, on which we lived. I have hated canned food ever since.

It was very sad, and sadder still to make them ready for their graves when they died. The poisoned arrows were almost always fatal, and caused great suffering. They knew however they would have a soldier's funeral, even in that distant desert; and although I had not a flower or even a green leaf to lay on their coffin they knew I would do what I could, and it pleased them. Yet I could only make them shabby little crosses of the scrubby grey Manzanita; and with difficulty get enough even of that. Still the living felt the dead were cared for, and the dying knew it would be so. But, oh the sadness, the pathetic nature of a soldier's funeral in that dreary desert.

As they sounded the three taps over the grave, it seemed to say they were called home for the last time and so far away from their native land. You know the taps are what call them into camp at night fall! . . . they gave those three taps softly, so softly, as a farewell, and left him there, under that blue broad sky and amidst those wide sandy deserts.

The other officer's wife at Camp McDowell, who Julia did not identify by name, was, according to Julia, mentally unstable. She recounted a story the woman told about her troubles that seemed to escalate the longer she stayed in the wild, barren desert:

Brave, oh no, she was the most nervous person I ever saw. Poor thing, she had suffered in early life a fearful shock from which she had never really recovered. I had noticed that she never would sit with a window behind her, nor if she could avoid it, would she allow anyone to pass at the back of her chair; she always tried to set it against a wall; and even then was continually glancing round first one shoulder then over the other, as if she feared some dreadful thing was there to attack her a l'improviste [unexpectedly or without warning]. . . .

[I]t was long before she came to Arizona; before she married in fact. Once at Washington, in a hotel; whilst preparing for bed, she had been startled by a conviction some one was watching her, and turning round in some alarm, she perceived a frightful man's face pushed in through the open transom over the door. Her terrified screams brought her friends from their rooms near hers, who found her insensible on her bed: a brain fever followed and it was weeks before she recovered consciousness enough to state what had alarmed her.

When her memory returned she explained it, but I fancy they mostly thought it a delusion. One thing was certain; her health and spirits both suffered, and she never recovered the shock. She could not bear to be in a room where there was a transom light, nor even to sit with her back to a window; and she continued so shaken that when she married an officer ordered to California the physicians had all agreed it would be the best thing for her to make a sea voyage to recover her health.

Unfortunately whilst on the passage she saw, or believed she saw amongst the forward passengers the very face which a year or two before had glared at her from above her door. The shock produced a fit which alarmed her husband and all her companions, but the captain was unable to discover the object of her fear. Still she persisted that she had actually seen the face, and she could not bear to go on deck, or even to be left alone in her berth, from dread.

If I remember rightly it appeared once more glaring in upon her in her state room, when her screams brought assistance, and he was actually traced. I rather think the Captain persuaded her to overlook the steerage passengers from the deck when they came for their dinner, and she pointed out the man, who then confessed that he had been the cause of her alarm; and that he had recognized her at once as the girl on whom he had played a trick in the Washington Hotel. I believe I am right so far. At least I am certain of the fact that the shocks were painfully real in their affects, and had left an impression from which she had never recovered. . . .

[F]righted as I was when the Indians were in camp her terrors were infinitely worse; and the agonies she suffered when her husband went scouting were really so terrible, that the efforts to comfort her used to do me good, I think; it was an occupation. It is always rather a support to find some one more unreasonably frightened even than oneself, and really in comparison with her I was brave.

In February 1870, after five months at Camp McDowell, Murray was ordered to Fort Yuma on detached service, and eventually rejoined his company at Fort Craig, New Mexico Territory. Julia and her son returned to California. "[I]t was impossible for me to accompany him," she said, "so I was forced to return to Oakland. My own family had come back from Europe, and under the escort of a brother officer of my husbands [sic] we once more crossed the desert, and came back to civilized life."

Julia's account concludes with the interviewer still filled with questions, but since her subject was tiring, she decided to wait until another time to continue the discussion. "That meeting however was not destined to take place," the interviewer wrote. "Three days afterward, with pansies braided in her beautiful golden hair, and violets placed between her crossed hands, she was laid in her coffin. The call for her had come, and she went where she would fear no more the heat of the sun."

At age twenty-four, on January 8, 1873, Julia died. The cause of her death is not known.

Murray Davis eventually left the Army and became Superintendent of the San Francisco Mint. He was later purportedly confirmed as Minister to China, but as he prepared for his new post, he suffered a serious illness and died July 25, 1877, only thirty-eight years old.

Young Stanton, five years old when his mother died and age nine when his father passed away, was adopted by Julia's family and remained with them until adulthood. Assuming his mother's family name, Stanton Davis Kirkland became a well-known naturalist, philosopher, ornithologist, and author. Unlike his parents, he lived a long, prosperous life, and died at age 76 in 1944.

CHAPTER 3

I Make It a Point to See All Worth Seeing

Mary Henrietta Banks Stacey

Mary Stacey loved to travel. By the time she arrived in Arizona Territory, she claimed she had made the trip across the continent six times, and her journeys were not yet at an end. She was an astute observer of her surroundings and an avid recorder of the terrain she covered. Mary often wrote to her mother about her adventures, the places she saw and the people she met. In turn, her mother sent Mary's letters to the local newspaper so that others could read her daughter's descriptions of the unique flora and fauna she encountered, and the events surrounding her ventures, particularly in Arizona's weird and wonderful desert wilderness.

Petite, golden-haired Mary Henrietta Banks was born in 1846 in Hollidaysburg, Pennsylvania, a small town east of Pittsburg and just south of Altoona. She believed she was a descendent of English soldier and statesman Oliver Cromwell, even naming one of her children after the parliamentarian, although the lineage is unsubstantiated.

At the age of twenty-three, on December 9, 1869, Mary married soldier May Humphreys Stacey, who enjoyed travel as much as his bride. Both husband and wife were short in stature, earning May Humphreys the nickname "the little colonel" within the family but certainly not on the battlefield.

May performed valiantly during the Civil War, receiving a bullet in his side that he carried the rest of his life. Yet even before he earned his stripes, May experienced an adventure few could duplicate.

In 1857, at the age of nineteen, May joined an expedition under the direction of Lieutenant Edward Fitzgerald Beale to survey a road from

Mary Henrietta Banks Stacey circa 1880s Arizona Historical Society, Photos-Stacey, Col. & Mrs. M. Humphreys #14377

New Mexico Territory to California that would cross through what would eventually become Arizona Territory. The remarkable element of this venture entailed herding a caravan of camels across the desert, an experiment Congress had authorized to determine if the military could use camels in lieu of horses and mules.

May kept a journal of his time with the camels and expressed his concern that the endeavor would not succeed since the camels were expected to carry extremely heavy loads, making them exceedingly slow. Plus, they frightened the horses and mules. But the major factor in the failure of the camel venture was the onset of the Civil War. No one had the time nor the patience to handle and train the new beasts of burden. After the war, the increase in rail travel made the camels obsolete.

Most of the camels were sold off, although up until the late 1890s, a few of the animals could be found roaming the Arizona desert.

After the Civil War, May continued his career with the Army. He was on leave from his post at Arizona's Fort Mohave along the Colorado River when he and Mary married. He assumed command of the post upon returning with his new bride, although Mary was back in Pennsylvania by November 1870, where she gave birth to her first child, Delilah Van Dycke Stacey.

May was ordered to Angel Island, California, in 1871. Mary joined him and gave birth to son Aubrey Banks Stacey at the California post in 1872. The family relocated to Nevada's Camp McDermit that same year, where they remained until May was ordered to return to Arizona as commander of Fort Thomas. While at Camp McDermit, Mary gave birth to her third child, Edward Cecil Cromwell Stacey, named after her presumed ancestor, Oliver Cromwell.

The Staceys enjoyed leave at home in Pennsylvania before heading out for Fort Thomas in 1878. May requested they be allowed to go by way of Panama this time instead of overland, the mode of travel they usually took, as it was less expensive and he now had not only his wife but three young children to transport. His request was granted.

Mary's initial letter or letters to her mother have not been found. However, most of her subsequent correspondence, which the *Altoona* (Pennsylvania) *Tribune* ran starting in November 1878, describes the family's journey after they arrived at Aspinwall (now Colón) before heading across the Isthmus of Panama. As her letters revealed, Mary encountered a variety of cultural diversities and her correspondence expressed many of the biases and prejudices of the day.

The newspaper sometimes used Mary's maiden name as the byline in her articles (Miss Mary Banks), and on other occasions, they credited the articles as written by Mrs. Col. Stacy, misspelling her last name. One of the first of her newspaper missives bears the date of Friday, November 1, 1878.

"Owing to the lateness of the hour of our arrival [in Aspinwall]," Mary wrote, "we shall be compelled to remain on board of ship all night. After dinner the Captain invited us and others to take a promenade on shore, which we were glad to do. The Captain led the procession up Main street, passing the innumerable drinking saloons in front of which men were playing écarté, rouge et noir [both French gaming activities], monte and other gambling games. We inspected by the light of a dim lantern the statue of Columbus, marking the spot where he first set foot upon the continent of America. Columbus stands with his left arm and hand extended, while his right arm is embracing an Indian girl, who seems to be partially shrinking from him. This fine piece of work stands on a rickety wooden base about three feet above the ground, the people of this wretched town being too poor or indifferent to supply it with anything more suitable."

The following morning, the family boarded the train that would take them from Aspinwall to the city of Panama. Mary, who had been brought up in an affluent household, noted, "The cars are small and such as would be used for third-class passengers in the United States. The locomotives are managed by natives. We ran about twenty miles an hour which is quite as fast as is safe over the track, which is not in very good condition. The road was mostly through a jungle beside the Chagres river, a small stream about 50 or 75 yards wide, now somewhat increased since the rainy season. The entire extent of the road across the isthmus, from ocean to ocean and from Aspinwall to Panama, is 47 1/2 miles. We passed several settlements, the houses being of the most primitive description, built of poles with high-peaked thatched roofs. The people loaf around doing nothing as though it were a perpetual Sunday."

As they sailed out of Panama, Mary noted a large school of porpoises just before arriving at Punta Arenas, Chile. From Chile, the ship traveled on to San José de Guatemala and Acapulco. Reaching Acapulco, she joined a group who left the ship to explore the area. Upon their return, she was told the ship's captain wished to speak to her. The report she wrote indicates the captain thought quite highly of Mary:

Just before leaving Acapulco the Captain had occasion to put a steerage passenger in irons for being drunk and disorderly and using abusive and threatening language to him and the other officers of the ship. In the evening he requested me to see the man, who was handcuffed to the iron grating just forward of the smokestack, and ascertain whether he was sober and whether in my judgment it would be prudent to release him from confinement, and also whether he was ready and willing to make an apology for his disreputable conduct. I did as requested, found the young man sober and willing to do anything to make amends. I told the Captain, who then desired me to see a Mr. Russell—a minister on board—and whatever we recommended he would do. I consulted the minister, making known to him the

captain's desire, but he declined to interfere, at the same time
saying he would not consider himself safe were the man liberated.
The Captain, however, released the man after he had apologized
to him and his first officer.

On November 14, Mary recorded that San Francisco was in "full view." "Voyage over, thank God," she wrote. "From here we continue our trip overland, seven hundred miles, to our post in Arizona."

From San Francisco, the Staceys traveled by train to Fort Yuma, a relatively new mode of transportation in that part of the West. Her report detailing this leg of the trip also appeared in the *Altoona Tribune*.

"The view of the Colorado desert is striking, as we speed on by rail," she wrote, "stretching off toward the south, apparently a limitless plain bounded only by the horizon; not a bush or tree to be seen."

As the train progressed through the desert, Mary remembered the trip she had taken seven years before when she came to Fort Mohave by Army ambulance.

The remarkable purity of the air permits very small objects to be
distinctly seen at a great distance, and gives wonderful coloring
to the distant objects. I also saw the phenomena of the mirage,
which has been so often described by travelers on the African
desert. Here we have it on a grand scale. Sometimes it takes the
form of a large fresh water lake. We hurry on to give our horses
water, and find the same smooth sand and polished pebbles we
left behind. Again we see tall mountains with overhanging prec-
ipices and spires and domes of buildings. We travel on, but all
have vanished from the air.

According to Mary, "Fort Huma [Yuma] lies on a butte or knob of granite one hundred feet above the Colorado river, which washes its base."

On the west the desert runs off toward the Pacific; on the south, the Colorado river stretching to the gulf; on the north, the river in its sinuous bed comes down from the distant mountains; on the east, we have a fine view from the Gila river and valley and of Arizona city, which is now quite a nice town. [The town of Yuma was first called Colorado City, then Arizona City until 1873, when the name was officially changed to Yuma.] I recall very vividly when we were here in 1870, on our way to Camp Mohave where Colonel Stacey was then in command, and which lies two hundred miles up the river from here, that I stood on the hill I have just described and witnessed the burial of a soldier.

Fort Yuma's commanding officer, Captain David Johnson Craigie, welcomed the Staceys to the outpost and offered his house for the night. "It is delightful here," Mary continued,

The thermometer is 80 in the sun, and we have all varieties of fruits and vegetables—strawberries, grapes, melons, cucumbers, green corn, tomatoes, etc. In front of these quarters is a fine yard with a fountain always playing; cactus ten feet high, a fine swing and croquet ground. In the garden are oranges, lemons, pomegranates, etc. . . . While I write the rail cars are passing over the bridge in front of me. Three steamers are lying in sight and a circus is expected. Do you want greater evidence of civilization and culture? Yet I can see the Indian fires opposite my windows and hear the cayotes [coyotes] cry at night. Strange juxtaposition. . . .

There were six hundred Chinese came in the cars with us to work on the railroad now being made up the Gila valley. One hundred and fifty miles is nearly completed to Maricopah [Maricopa] wells. It is said these Chinese will lay two miles of rail a day.

Colonel Stacey brought with us sixty soldiers to act as guard on our trip. We will in a few days say good-by to Fort Huma, and with ambulance, wagons and soldiers start for Fort Thomas, five hundred miles distant. Will go by Tucson, and will write you from there. We are all well, and anticipate many novel sights on our overland trip.

Mary's next correspondence appeared in the *Tribune* under the title "Over the Colorado Desert," detailing the company as they departed Fort Yuma:

Our outfit . . . consisted of two immense prairie schooners with twelve mules each, an ambulance with four horses, with a Spanish driver, named Don Alfera, a fine specimen of Mexican driver, who speaks only Spanish. We have seventy-nine soldiers, who are compelled to travel on foot, as the government made no provision for their transportation. "No appropriation by Congress," was the cry when Colonel Stacy [the newspaper misspelled the last name] telegraphed for wagons for these men. We halted over night only four miles out, so as to be sure we had all things needful for our journey.

Lieutenant [Millard Fillmore] Waltz and his wife [Corrie], who is a young lady from Maryland, is a bride, and this is her first experience of army life. Brother Dave Stacy [May Stacey's brother], of San Francisco, who is going to see the gold mines in this region, nurse [Rose was the children's nurse] and the children, D.M. Alfera and I are in the ambulance. Colonel Stacy rides on horseback so that he can superintend the movements of the cavalcade. We have four large tents, and each soldier has what they call an A tent.

November 28—We took breakfast by star light; had fresh biscuit, beefsteak and good coffee, jellies, etc. "Chandler" is our cook. He was with us at Camp Halleck in 1875, and Colonel Stacy brought him with us from San Francisco. We arrived at this place at noon; it is called Paplos station. We are in view of the railroad to Tucson up the Gila river. The rails have been laid, and the track cars are running. Chinamen are working hard on the road ahead of us.

We started early this morning hoping to get to Gila city in time to camp. When we got here we found Gila city consisted of two buildings and an Indian hut.

Established around 1858, Gila City lay on the south side of the Gila River, which the troops followed for a good distance. The caravan had now traveled almost twenty-five miles from Fort Yuma but there was little to keep them at the old stage stop except a few adobe houses and possibly a saloon or two.

"Have not seen a white woman since we left Yuma," Mary continued. They reached Mission Camp the next day, another old stage station. "Colonel Stacy telegraphed to Yuma for new teams and drivers and they arrived to-day. Aubrey and I are quite sick drinking the alkali water. On Sunday we reached Fillibuster at 1 o'clock. This is a stage station. Two very nice little girls came down to our camp to see the children, and as I was not well I did not go down to the station. We got milk and mutton from these folks, paying well for both."

Since it was Sunday, Mary gave a Bible lesson to the little girls along with her own children. "I had my pocket testament, given to me by Mr. Joseph Smith, of Hollidaysburg, as a Christmas gift when I was a very little girl, just learning to read."

Monday, December 2—We were up by daylight and reached Salt Laguna (lake) at 1 o'clock. Here we found an empty adobe house. We went in for shade and found the oyers [ollas or clay pots] filled with good cold water. We were fearfully hot and dusty, and after indulging in what ablutions we could, I put on a fresh white muslin dress and felt rejuvenated.

While here we were surprised by the arrival of an ox team with a Mexican and his wife and four babies, the oldest being only three years old. The youngest were twins. They wore little shirts like the colored children in the southern States wear. The woman wore sort of waist or skirt, with a long blue gingham scarf over her head—rebosa style [a woven scarf that covers the head and shoulders]. The wagon was wheels with boards over them, hay thrown on the boards, then the woman and babies; then perched on any and every available place were chickens. We found we were occupying their home and they had been out on a "pleasure" excursion. They only bowed their heads when they came up. We said, "Buenos dios." They smiled and said, "Buenos dios."

The woman took the babies and two dogs out of the wagon. One of the latter was a Chihuahua dog; it had no hair on it and looked like a big rat; its skin was mouse color. She went out under a porch with a brush roof; made a little fire; boiled some milk, and began feeding first a dog and then a baby, just as they yelled for it. I took her some loaf-cut sugar and added it to the milk, much to the delight of the babies at least.

She then prepared her husband's dinner in this way: She took some beef that had been dried in the sun, and putting it on a stone, pounded it with a smaller one. Then she made a stew of it, making it red with Chili pepper. Then she made a kind of pan cake of cornmeal, salt and water, which she called tortillas (pronounced tortages). This was all they had to eat after their long ride.

Having traveled sixty miles from Fort Yuma, the troops bedded down for the night at the stage post Mohawk, also south of the Gila River,

which had been established the previous year. A nearby rancher provided the troops with fresh meat along with barley and hay for the mules
and horses. Mary was pleased they had clear, clean drinking water at a
nearby well. And even out on the desolate plain, the ladies of the column
decided they had time to make a little molasses taffy.

"We had some trouble here," Mary reported, "some of the soldiers
stole the man's [rancher's] honey; he complained to Colonel Stacy who
at once sent Lieutenant Waltz to investigate the charge. He found they
had taken $5 worth; he made the men pay, so peace was restored."

*We rode next day through a beautiful canon called Teamster
Canon. We came to a house built of adobe and lined with
picture papers. The owner had oyers filled with good water.
Colonel Stacy had to buy water for his men and teams at a
dollar a barrel. Two men gave out and we had to leave them at
a station to recuperate.*

*After our tents were struck I made an excellent omelet of eggs
sent me by the man at the house. He said I was the nicest lady he
had met in the army. I presume officers' wives had offended him,
and as I talked to him he thought I was charming and sent me
all the eggs he had.*

*The soldiers who had walked are getting tired, so tired we
are much retarded on our journey. The station where we are now
stopping is kept by quite a nice Southern woman whose husband
is in the Legislature, and while she sells peach brandy and meat
to the soldiers, her husband makes the laws for the Territory. So
the world goes.*

On December 5, the company arrived at Burkes Station, although Mary
called it Buttes Station in her narrative. This was another stage stop
along the Yuma/Tucson Road. Opened in 1877, the station kept the

military telegraph line in repair. It was abandoned in 1880 when the railroad roared through the Arizona desert.

"From here," Mary wrote, "my command, that is, the ambulance, rode over the Gila river some six miles to the boiling springs."

Mary had arrived at Agua Caliente about three miles north of the Gila River. The hot, bubbling baths had been used since the mid 1700s by local Indians to ease their tired bodies after a long ride. "We heard of these springs as soon as we reached the buttes," Mary wrote. "So I concluded I would go at once. Brother Dave Colonel Stacy would not go. I make it a point to see all worth seeing as I travel. It was a dusty ride, but we were fully compensated for it. The water was bubbling out of the ground hot and soft. Rose bathed the children, and Lieutenant and Mrs. Waltz and I took baths in a bath house made from brush. The water was up to our arms. It was delightful."

As they passed ancient petroglyphs carved in sandstone, Mary described the engraved drawings that have their origins with Native peoples

Agua Caliente Arizona Historical Society, Buehman-Places-Agua Caliente, #32538

who roamed the territory many years before the white man arrived. She was ignorant of the convictions and moralities of these societies.

"Birds, beasts, figures of all kinds, even the cross is cut in it," she wrote. "The cross! This sacred emblem of Christian faith and salvation. By whom had it been cut and for what purpose! Surely not as a symbol of their belief in Christ, for how had these ancient people learned of our Savior or his atonement? We contemplated the mysterious hieroglyphics with awe and wonder."

As they drove on to Oatman Flat, about eighteen miles east of Agua Caliente, Mary recalled the massacre of the Oatman family, probably by Yavapai Apaches, that had occurred in 1851, and the captivity of thirteen-year-old Olive Ann Oatman and her eight-year-old sister Mary Ann. Mary Ann did not survive in captivity but Olive lived with her captors for about a year before being sold to the Mojaves who lived along the Colorado River. Five years after she had been taken, Olive was sold back to her people for the price of one horse. She was brought into Fort Yuma, where she was reunited with her brother who had survived the massacre. The rest of her family, except for little Mary Ann, are buried at Oatman Flat.

"We were here but a short time," Mary said. "Colonel Stacy said if he could have stopped long enough he would have had their graves marked with a better monument."

As Sunday morning, December 8, dawned, Mary remembered it was her ninth wedding anniversary. She also noted this was her seventh trip across the continent.

Arriving at the Gila Bend stage station, named after a sudden turn in the Gila River, Mary noted the weather was cooling off compared to when they set out from Fort Yuma. "We reached Happy camp [another stage station] today—so called, the man said, because here we could procure good water after our long dirty ride, and as our teams had not came up we made a bed for our little Cromwell, who complained of the cold. I am afraid he will not have the power of endurance of his great progenitor, Oliver Cromwell."

Mary watched as, "Wagon after wagon passed here on their way from Tucson to Yuma, twelve or fifteen oxen hitched to each wagon and the men swearing and whipping them in such a dreadful manner that it made one sick. Profanity wafted to our ears by the pure midnight air seemed like curses on this country."

We arrived at Maricopah [Maricopa] Wells today; here we found good water—aqua dulce it is called in Spanish. It is quite cold to night, ice forming in our tents. The poor soldiers feel it. It was hot in Yuma and they sold their overcoats and blankets. Many of them are foot sore and shoeless, as the department furnished no supplies at Yuma.

As they pulled into the Montezuma stage stop, Mary found it a "pleasant place."

Here we found a good store, and Mr. Dempsey who keeps it has a charming wife; a fine home filled with nice furniture and articles of beauty and value like our eastern homes. We here met with a new ambulance from Camp Thomas. We gave our old one to some sick soldiers, which gave me great pleasure to see them thus cared for.

The store here was finer than any country store I had ever seen in the east. We all got weighed. The children had gained in their trip, and the nurse fifteen pounds. I, who had the mental labor, had lost several pounds.

Mr. Dempsey gave me some pottery, one a broken bowl he had dug out fourteen feet under ground, when he was digging his cellar. How many years it had laid there, who can tell, or by whom made? He also gave me some Arizona rubies [probably garnet gemstones that can be found throughout Arizona], very bright which will be handsome when dressed and set.

Mrs. Dempsey gave me a beautiful bowl made by Pimo [Pima] Indians, who have a village here. We went to visit them. Their houses look like the pictures of the Esquimaux [Inuit or Eskimo people] huts, but instead of snow theirs are made of mud and look like an inverted crock, with one opening for a door. They were all sitting out doors. The women had on calico skirts, flowing from the waist down; shoulders and head bare. The children with their little shirts on looked like the Maricopa Indians. I tried to trade with them, but succeeded in getting only one dish for fifty cents. They are hard to trade with. You have to pretend you don't want the article, and then they are anxious enough to barter or sell.

These Pimo Indians have farms, and we saw a school house where they are taught by the Jesuit Fathers. Mrs. Dempsey took us to see a chief who supplied her husband with grain in exchange for his goods. We found the old chief dressed in white drawers or pantaloons with a gray blanket thrown around him, sitting on a rude bench with his grandchild on his knee under a rude porch or shelf. There are many other huts around, in which his sons and their families dwell, all working under him as the slaves did in the South under an overseer.

One quite pretty woman was grinding corn on a large stone, rubbing it with a smaller end. Another was cooking "frijoles," a kind of Mexican bean. All speak Spanish. These women were his daughters-in-law. He sent a "muchancho" [sic] (boy) after his son, who was working in a field close by. When he came we found him a fine-looking young Indian. Mrs. Dempsey asked him if he would give us some music. He brought out of his hut a harp *which he had made himself. He made very sweet music, indeed, playing waltzes in a minor key. We ladies took a waltz, much to the amusement of these people.*

We then said "adios" and went to see an old woman making oyers for holding water. The material of which these vessels are made is clay—formed by hand and are in the shape of an urn with a top, but have no bottom upon which to stand. A rope or leather strap is tied around the neck and they are suspended from the side of a wall, or the ceiling of a hut. The vessel being porous, the water in it evaporates rapidly, and what remains is as cold as ice water. . . .

The ruins of Cassa [Casa] Grande, which lie three miles from this place, is a celebrated ruin of the ancient cliff dwellers. We said good-by to Mr. and Mrs. Dempsey and started for the ruins. We traveled through a cloud of alkali dust, saw some fine mesquite trees covered with mistletoe with bright red berries. In the distance is Santa Catalina mountains, said to be filled with minerals. We found Cassa Grande only walls; the floor and roof had fallen in.

Why Mary thought the ruins had been inhabited by cliff dwellers is curious, since there is little terrain in the area to support houses built into rocks. Surrounded by miles of timeworn irrigation ditches created and used by ancient civilizations such as the Hohokam, who farmed in the Arizona desert, Casa Grande today is a national monument under the protection of the National Parks Service.

From Casa Grande, the entourage made its way a short distance to the Picacho stage station. Informed the stage keeper at Picacho was a disagreeable fellow, Mary set out to charm him.

Chanalas, the cook, came to me and said, "This man has fresh meat but he won't sell any; eggs but says he don't like soldiers." So I went into the house ostensibly to warm; at first he would not look at me, but I talked to him and petted his dog and he relented enough to smile at me. Colonel Stacy came in at this time and said, "This man looks like a murderer." But I seemed to have touched some good chord in his heart, for he sent me ten dozen fresh eggs, and said, "invite the lady down to the house and I will make a big fire." I went to bed feeling very sorry for that man, as I had been told his wife was dead, and I saw an empty cradle in his house.

"We are only nine miles from Tucson," Mary exclaimed, "and we are about to encamp for the night. Just saw a hawk fly away with a large snake in its claws, and also a beautiful scarlet bird called the Tucson oriole. The next day we drove through Tucson to Camp Lowell. We are now three hundred miles on our way and the rest of the journey is said to be very pleasant traveling. After breakfasting we drove into Tucson to make some purchases."

Our way now tends up hill and north from Tucson. We can see miles and miles of desert lying west of us. We can see Camp Grant just at the foot of the mountain. We saw the most superb mirage to-day. A fine lake with the shadows mirrored on its depths, rocks hanging over the edges and picturesque islands lying at the foot of Tombstone mountain, and that was an illusion produced by the highly refractory air of this climate. Immense quantities of gold and silver are found in this mountain, and much immigration is now taking place.

As Christmas approached and Mary found herself almost to her new home, she asked the soldiers to stop and cut down a tree so her children would have something to put their presents under once they settled at Camp Thomas.

Arriving at the post on December 23rd, Mary, who had followed the Gila River across most of the territory, mistakenly thought she was now at the headwaters of the rambling watercourse, but the Gila flows out of western New Mexico before entering Arizona Territory.

"Captain [Augustus G.] Tassin of the Twelfth infantry is here with his company of Indian scouts," Mary reported. "They look very picturesque; wear soldier trowsers [sic], dark blue coats and large black felt hats. Captain Tassin has given them a long red flannel scarf which is tied on their hats; it is showy. And he can distinguish his Indians at a great distance. Colonel [William L.] Foulk commands the cavalry, but as Colonel Stacy is the ranking officer he commands the post."

Two days later, the Christmas tree served its purpose as the family gathered underneath its piney boughs to exchange gifts. Unfortunately, Mary found a less cheerful mission for the tree's remains.

"One of the soldiers, who was on guard, accidentally shot himself," she said. "I took the tree and made a cross of it. His coffin was wrapped in a flag and the cross placed on his coffin—a cross made from a Christmas tree—symbol [of] our faith, and buried with honor in honor of the brave, and I trust, good man, who fell in his line of duty. May we all be found at our post fully equipped for the long march to the happy hunting ground."

As winter turned to spring and summer brought the heat of the desert to Camp Thomas, Colonel Stacey suggested the family take a trip up nearby Mount Graham, which rises to an elevation of over 10,000 feet, to cool off for a few days. Soldiers were headed into the mountains to chop down trees for construction of new living quarters at the post. And although Mary dreaded "bumping in an ambulance," she loved to travel and agreed the trip would be a nice break from the monotony of post life.

Along with the three Stacey children, Nurse Rose and the cook also joined the camping expedition. As was her practice, Mary described to her mother all she witnessed on the excursion. This letter, however, was not published in the newspaper but kept by the family until 1950, when it was turned over to the Arizona Historical Society Museum in Tucson.

"After preparing a bushel of green tomatoes and a bushel of cucumbers in salt for pickles to be ready when we come back for the vinegar," Mary wrote, "I packed up clothes, bedding, etc.—One does not know how many things are positively necessary to one's comfort until they start to travel."

It was "don't forget the dutch oven, be sure you have plenty of towels, is my tooth brush in, get plenty of blankets as it will be cold. Take warm clothes for the children. Though the thermometer is 108 here, it will be very low in the mountains. Send to the hospital for ammonia and quinine, to the sutlers for whiskey in case of snakebite, to the commissary for can[ned] tomatoes, peaches, pears, pickles, crackers, oysters, clams, turtle soup, condensed milk, flour, etc." One would think Col. S. was going to live some time among the mountains.

The sergeant has charge of the soldiers and their rations and they have their cook. At half past two o'clock we pulled out with four six-mule teams, an ambulance and 12 men . . . One waggon [sic] has our bedding, tents, and trunks, five camp chairs, folding table, etc. We had just gotten out of camp when a double tree [crossbar used in harnessing animals] on the waggon broke, two front mules ran off. Back flew the orderly. Within a few minutes a new double tree was brought from camp, and fixed on, and away we bumped.

That evening, they stayed in the little community of Cottonwood. "Our tents up carpeted with canvas, my cot with a good hair mattress, clean white sheets and pillows with heavy white mission blankets bordered with blue. Looked very inviting. Brussels carpet, camp chairs, trunk and dressing case with hanging glass looked quite like living, and very cozy."

The next morning, Mary felt ill and suspected she was suffering from malaria, a common ailment among soldiers and civilians in southeastern Arizona. By noon they were about fifteen miles west of Fort Grant in Eureka Springs at the cattle ranch of the Leitch brothers—Mary misspelled their name as Leech—who provided lunch for the group.

She told her mother, "Aubrey rode a little burro (mule) and Delia a horse for an hour or so in the courtyard. As it was so warm this morning I put all heavy wraps in the trunk. In half an hour after leaving Eureka a heavy storm came up. It thundered and the rain poured down. . . . We now rode for several hours in a very cold damp state, no shawls no coats, etc. This is the most uncertain country you ever saw. When we left Eureka no signs of rain—in half an hour a dreadful storm. We rode up and up and at half past six o'clock we were in the canon and made camp. It had ceased raining but everything was wet."

The cook prepared dinner, which was "eaten by lantern lights and big fires in a canon where Indians hide, where an immense bear was killed last week by a soldier. We had ditches dug around the tents in case it rained in the night—as the sky looked very black. One double-barrel shotgun, one rifle, and two revolvers are loaded and by our beds in case of trouble for who knows what might come."

This morning, Monday, we rise to a bright sun, no more rain. After a nice warm breakfast with warm flannel cakes [pancakes], we took a look around. Found the most beautiful flowers. I send you some of the Spanish bayonet fruit and flower. A prickly pear apple which looks like a crimson Easter egg is very pleasant eating—a little acid—one has to be very careful of the prickles. . . . Delia gathered a little tin bucket of wild grapes which Rose

stewed for lunch. They were delicious—tart and so fresh. . . . I
am much better today. I have been shooting at target. . . .
The children are as busy as bees. They have a camp fire of
their own and are playing emigrants, cooking meat, making
soup and toast. . . . The children are perfect nomads and love this
kind of life. . . . Rose and the children saw a large black bear this
morning on the hillside but the Col. and his men were up after
the rest of the logs so there was no Bar hunt.

Knowing they would pass close to Camp Grant, Mary had planned
ahead and brought along proper clothing in case they decided to go
onto the post. Since there were several officers' wives at Grant, she
wanted to be dressed properly to call on them. And although envious
of the quarters at Grant compared to the housing at Camp Thomas, she
was not at all impressed with the women she met. "I should put new life
in them," she said. "[They] are all so stupid."

They spent the night at Eureka Springs and set off for Cottonwood
the next day. As they left Cottonwood, "we met a Mexican circus on
their way to Camp Grant. They had showed at Camp Thomas last night.
There were several wagons, horses and camels raised from the stock
Col. Stacey had helped to bring in with Gene Beale in '57. Some were
lost in western Arizona, these raised from them."

Young Aubrey did not feel well the last 25 miles back to Camp
Thomas. A weary Mary wrote as she closed her letter, "As it was very
hot and I nursed him, holding a basin in one hand, you can imagine I
was very tired when we arrived at Thomas. We had ridden 35 miles in
one day over hills such as you have never seen. . . . Mrs. Lt. Allen had a
fine dinner awaiting us but the children and I went to bed at once after
a plunge bath. The dust had been so heavy and thick we could not have
shut our eyes without a bath."

Mary and her family remained in Arizona until 1882, when her husband was relocated. During those years, May also served some time on the San Carlos Indian Reservation and at Fort Lowell.

While at Fort Lowell, Mary had the opportunity to entertain General William Tecumseh Sherman, who not only distinguished himself during the Civil War but became Commanding General of the Army from 1869 until 1883 and spent several years in the West during the Indian Wars. At a luncheon she hosted for the general, Mary presented him with a life-sized replica of the head of Apache chief Juh that she had made in repoussé (hammered) copper. "The work has been greatly admired and shows great talent," reported the April 22, 1882, *Army and Navy Journal*. "The likeness to the old desperado is excellent. Mrs. Stacey had nothing to guide her but her recollections of the Indian, having seen him once at Fort Thomas, Arizona."

Another of Mary's talents was palmistry with which she often entertained the men at the forts. She was also an avid student of astronomy.

On February 12, 1886, Mary's world came crashing in around her when her husband of seventeen years died suddenly while on post at Fort Ontario, New York, succumbing to the wounds he had suffered during his Civil War service. Mary received a monthly pension of twenty dollars, plus two dollars for each of her children, who were all still quite young. And although her widow's pension was eventually raised to thirty dollars a month, she had little other income upon which to exist.

Sixteen-year-old Delilah, determined to help support her mother and younger brothers, set out on a career in acting. She did quite well in the theater but is remembered more as the first woman to smoke a cigarette on a New York streetcar. And although there was no law against a woman smoking on streetcars, newspapers reported that other women passengers "showed signs of apoplexy" as a result of Delilah's conduct.

Little is known of Aubrey Stacey's life except he followed his father into the Army, as did his younger brother Edward. Edward was recognized for his bravery under fire as well as inventing and patenting a combined waterproof cape, blanket, and shelter tent for military use.

For many years, Mary moved from town to town but mainly resided in New York City, living in boarding houses, and may have spent some years teaching at a private school in the city. Despite her financial woes, she remained active in social organizations such as the Manhattan Mystic Lodge, which tended to the needs of military Mason families who were injured during the war. She was also a member of New York's Rainy Day Club and protested the inclusion of women in short dresses for a social event at the Waldorf Astoria Hotel in 1898. As reported in *The World* newspaper, Mary argued, "Short dress is undress. You might as well ask a man to go to dinner in a morning suit as want us to attend a euchre party in—in curtailment." An argument ensued but, in the end, long skirts were considered the only proper attire for the day.

When she died on January 21, 1918, seventy-one-year-old Mary was living with Delilah in Evanston, Illinois; son Edward was stationed at nearby Fort Sheridan. Her estate consisted of about one hundred dollars and a few personal effects that were in storage in New York City. Mary had few material goods to show for all her travels but no one could take away her memories.

PART II

Post Life

W hen it came time to move to the next post, the allotted one thousand pounds of furniture and necessary goods meant countless items had to be left behind. Although furniture was a scarcity on the frontier, it was also a heavy burden to tote from one fort to the next. Women sold what they could with the hope of finding replacements wherever they were sent. Instead, what they usually found upon arrival were crudely built tables and upturned barrels as substitutes for chairs. A bed might be constructed by placing a board across a couple of crates. Clothing was hung on nails hammered into walls.

Flooring was often nonexistent in post housing. Dirt floors were covered with straw before army blankets or animal furs were laid down and nailed to wall bases. If one was lucky enough to have a wooden floor, the planks might be so warped that any little thing dropped usually disappeared under the house. Snakes, tarantulas, scorpions, and centipedes lived under these insecure floorboards. The Corbusier family stuffed their shoes with paper every evening to prevent snakes from curling up inside.

Forrestine Cooper Hooker, who lived a good portion of her childhood on military forts across the Southwest, remembered the home she and her parents occupied in the Chiricahua Mountains at Camp Bonita in 1885. The house, which consisted of one room, was certainly cozy, and to the delight of Forrestine and her father, all the walls were decorated with newspaper. The two often competed to find articles on the walls the other had not yet read.

"I would climb onto a chair to read some fresh item located near the ceiling," Forrestine said, "and after I had read it aloud, would turn

A little fun at Fort Grant circa 1890s; group of soldiers and families sitting on and around a carriage at Fort Grant (Ariz.) during Indian Wars in Arizona AZ State Library, Archives, and Public Records, History and Archives Division, Phoenix, #96-3226

to see my father's six-foot, two-inch frame flattened on the floor as he answered my challenge by saying, 'That's not new. I read that long ago, but here's something you have missed.' Then he would triumphantly read an item located at the junction of the wall and floor."

One of the most frustrating aspects of moving to a new fort was the uncertainty of acquiring suitable housing as well as keeping it until ordered elsewhere. A recently arrived higher-ranking officer could claim the residence of a junior officer and the ousted family had only a day or two to relocate to a dwelling of lesser desirability. Except for the commanding officer, no one was immune from losing their home.

Fanny Corbusier first experienced the ritual of ranking out when her husband was ordered from Fort Bowie to Fort Grant in 1884. Having acquired the best quarters for her family, right next to the commanding officer's house, Fanny set to work making the large residence comfortable and homey. No sooner did she feel settled in her new surroundings than a higher-ranking officer arrived at the post, forcing the Corbusiers out of their tidy dwelling into a less desirable one that Fanny described as an old "large, ugly stone structure," one of the first houses built on the post.

The following year, the family found more suitable quarters and moved into an adobe structure but were soon turned out again. They finally acquired housing in which they remained for the rest of their time at the fort. All of this moving, readjustment, and redecorating took a toll on the entire household.

When a new officer and his wife arrived, their first obligation was to pay a call on the commander, who went to considerable trouble to obtain the finest foods he could acquire to entertain the newcomers. The latest arrivals might be wined and dined with champagne, hors d'oeuvres, and a feast of imported delicacies from the West Coast, all served on a table complete with damask cloth, fine china and silverware, although the table itself might be made of a wooden board laid across a couple of carpenter's horses.

These social gatherings continued until every officer had hosted the latest family. The new family was then obligated to reciprocate in kind.

Entertaining was a constant and important part of maintaining one's standing at a post, and woe to the officer who failed to initiate and return these social visits—his chance for advancement greatly diminished.

The wife played a central role at these societal gatherings. Through her associations with other officers' wives, she could help promote her husband's career, learn about upcoming promotions, know when troops were moving out, and brag about her spouse's merits.

The commanding officer's wife, known as the K.O.W. (rather than C.O.W. because of the connotation of the word "cow"), set the standards of social conduct on a post, and was the official hostess for visiting officers and civilians. If the post was large enough, she would oversee dances (also known as hops) and theatrical shows, organize picnics and outings, and was often the prime source of fort gossip.

Post life, however, could be tedious and boring for women. They wrote home complaining of loneliness and isolation, sometimes mentioning they were the only officer's wife on a post. They longed for female companionship and were delighted when a caravan appeared out of the desert bringing not only much-needed supplies but the chance that a woman might be on board.

To relieve the routine of post living, women played card games and held sewing bees. Fanny Corbusier enjoyed gardening. "We always planted something wherever we went," she said, "and left a post richer by trees, shrubs, and various other plants." At Arizona's Fort Grant, she produced a successful crop of peach trees.

Ellen Biddle busied herself at Fort Lowell raising chickens and turkeys, and bought three cows to provide fresh milk for her children.

Excursions beyond the protection of post guards were dependent upon the Indian situation in a region. Both men and women liked to ride and many officers' wives enjoyed fishing and hunting, particularly if wild game was plentiful. Visits to nearby friendly Indian villages afforded women the chance to see how Native peoples lived, broadening their perspectives about an often-maligned ominous foe. They wrote to their eastern relatives about Native lifestyles and customs. They admired and collected woven baskets, clay ollas, fine blankets, and brilliant silver crafted by divergent indigenous tribes.

Mail delivery to a post was sporadic; it might come once a week or every couple of months. Letters from home were read and re-read. Women subscribed to magazines and almost always had a stash of books buried beneath the wagonload of home goods that accompanied them.

Indian attacks and raids relentlessly preyed on the emotions of both soldiers and their spouses. Women did express curiosity about Native customs, dress, and activities yet when they visited nearby Indian encampments, they were always accompanied by a military escort. As a precaution, according to Ellen Biddle, "all the ladies in those days went out to target practice and were taught the use of firearms."

In 1875 when Lieutenant Jack Summerhayes received orders to relocate from Fort Apache to Camp McDowell, his wife Martha bundled up her newborn baby, fitted a small derringer around her waist, and boarded a wagon for the long journey. At one point, they had to maneuver through a pass notorious for concealing raiding Apaches. As they started through, Jack cautioned Martha that if he was shot, she should use the derringer on both her and the baby rather than be taken captive. "Don't let them get either of you alive," he warned. Martha clung to her baby as the wagon careened through the pass, not at all sure she could do as her husband requested if she was taken captive. Fortunately the pass lay empty. On the other side, Jack whipped out his flask and all enjoyed a good swig of whiskey.

* * *

Two women who spent several years in Arizona Territory left lasting recollections of the hardships as well as the delights they encountered while trying to maintain a comfortable home, rear children, and create a safe environment during their tenures living on rough, crudely built forts.

Frances Boyd's disastrous housing situation at Fort Whipple, and later at Camp Date Creek, demonstrates the trials of making a home in a desolate and unforgiving land. Yet Frances took it all in stride and often made fun of herself and her foibles as she traveled the vast, rugged West.

As had Martha Summerhayes, Sarah Upham gave birth to her first child at Fort Apache. Unlike Martha, Sarah left no record of her time in Arizona, yet her husband, Frank, was so proud of how his wife handled the threat of an Indian disturbance, an incident that could have turned into a desperate situation, that he lauded her abilities in an article published over ten years after they had left the territory. Frank's details of Camp Apache during their tenure are also noteworthy.

CHAPTER 4

No Woman Could Be Induced to Go to Arizona

Frances Anne Mullen Boyd

Eighteen-year-old Frances (Fannie) Anne Mullen met Orsemus Bronson Boyd in 1866 and had already heard the accusations surrounding his tenure at the United States Military Academy. But once she set eyes on this handsome, quiet man, all doubts of his innocence faded. They married October 9, 1867, and immediately set out for the western frontier, leaving behind Orsemus's troubled past.

Fannie had been born in New York City on February 14, 1848, and loved everything about the metropolis, insisting it was "the only habitable place on the globe." Coming from a well-to-do family (Fannie's father owned a popular bakery in the city), the idea of traveling across barren deserts, sleeping under the stars, and living in adobe housing probably never entered her mind until she fell in love with the Army man who transformed her life into one of undeniable hardship, but also filled it with deep devotion and love.

Orsemus Bronson Boyd had already distinguished himself serving two years with the Union Army before entering West Point at the age of eighteen in 1862. His brother Amos died during the war.

Orsemus was not a popular cadet and eventually, one of his classmates accused him of stealing money from another. Years later, the classmate confessed he had lied but by then, Orsemus had graduated and headed west, wanting no part of the disgrace he had endured at the hands of his peers.

Two days after their wedding, the newlyweds were on their way to San Francisco en route to their first assignment at Camp Halleck, Nevada, just north of present-day Elko. They traveled by way of the

Isthmus of Panama and Fannie found the three-week trip "delightful, and the change from bleak, cold winter to the tropical scenes of Panama, and thence to the soft and balmy air of the Pacific, was so exhilarating that travel was simply a continuous pleasure."

Fannie wrote of her western travels in her book, *Cavalry Life in Tent and Field*, published in 1894. The manuscript is a tribute to her husband and his distinguished career with the Army, but she also details her times and trials traipsing across deserts as well as up and down worrisome precipices, fretting about her children, trying to cook edible meals from meager offerings, and learning to cope with military life. She experienced new, sometimes perilous routes, particularly during her time in Arizona Territory. Occasionally, her sense of humor peeked out from these pages and doubtless alleviated her anxieties during those tumultuous years.

From San Francisco, the couple went by steamer to Sacramento, then by train to the tiny town of Cisco, California, where they encountered snow that led to travel by sled and stagecoach across mountainous ranges and dry desert into Nevada Territory.

Finally arriving at Nevada's Camp Halleck, Fannie discovered she and the Captain's wife were the only officers' wives at the fort.

Cooking, she said, "was simplified by absolute lack of materials," consisting mainly of bacon, flour, beans, coffee, tea, rice, and sugar, plus a handful of condiments. "Our only luxury was dried apples, and with these I experimented in every imaginable way until toward the last my efforts to disguise them utterly failed, and we returned to our simple rations."

She also learned to fish, which resulted in a modicum of variety on the dinner table. "With all its drawbacks," Fannie wrote, "life in the open air then began to have many charms for me."

The Boyds remained at Camp Halleck about a year before Orsemus, now at the rank of first lieutenant, was ordered to Prescott, Arizona

Territory. Fannie packed her scant belongings and prepared for the long journey before her. She was pregnant with her first child.

The couple went to California before crossing the desert into Arizona Territory. On March 16, 1869, Fannie gave birth to daughter, Mabel, in San Francisco.

The nurse hired to care for both her and the baby was anything but tender hearted, according to Fannie. "[M]y own sufferings were almost intolerable," she wrote, "while I felt sure the poor little baby was being continually dosed. The nurse weighed nearly three hundred pounds, and at night when she lay down beside me her enormous weight made such an inclined plane of the bed that I could not keep from rolling against her; and she snored so loudly that not only was it impossible for me to sleep, but for any one else on the same floor. The sounds were not at all sedative in their effects, and I spent the nights praying for morning."

Fannie and Orsemus finally decided they could do better caring for little Mabel on their own, but in their naiveté the poor child almost died when Fannie tried to give her an entire spoonful of paregoric to ease her crying. "Had not the drug in its raw strength nearly strangled her, we would, undoubtedly, have murdered our dear little infant."

Fannie confessed, "That was not the only experiment we tried and looking back I pity the poor child with all my heart. Our anxiety to improve her appearance was so great that whatever we were advised to do was attempted. I cut off baby's eyelashes one day to make them grow thicker; and when she was a little older, while we were in Arizona, I found her father pressing that dear little nose between the prongs of a clothespin to better its shape."

After purchasing supplies for the trip to Arizona, Fannie, Orsemus, and three-week-old Mabel boarded the train for Los Angeles. With them traveled their new servant, a twelve-year-old Chinese boy who, Fannie claimed, was the only person she could find to go with them because, "no woman could be induced to go to Arizona. First, because no church was there. Second, and mainly, because many Indians were."

The small two-seated wagon provided for the long journey had to hold all of their belongings:

A mattress and blankets were strapped on the back, and over those a chair. The inside was simply crowded with an array of articles demanded by our long journey. We had not only all necessary clothing, but as much food in a condensed shape as could be taken; there was no room for luxuries. Our first care was to be well armed, as we were going among hostile Indians, a fact I could scarcely realize; therefore our vehicle held, in addition to all else, a gun, two pistols, and strapped overhead my husband's two sabers, which he required when on duty. . . .

With my usual docility in accepting advice concerning baby, I had followed the suggestion of an army paymaster's wife, who considered a champagne basket the proper receptacle for an infant when traveling. Never was advice given which proved more useful or beneficial. If with all the other hardships of that journey I had been compelled to hold baby day after day, not only would I have been far more fatigued, but she far less comfortable. Cradled in that basket, the motion of our carriage acted as a perpetual lullaby, and the little one slept soundly all the time, waking only when progress ceased. The basket was tightly strapped to the front seat beside my husband, who drove, while I sat on the back one with our little Chinaman.

First stop for the troops was California's Camp Cady close to the present-day town of Barstow near the Mojave River. (According to popular lore, Mohave is spelled with an "h" east of the Colorado River [i.e., in Arizona], while in California it is spelled with a "j").

Upon leaving the small camp, the Boyds "found ourselves dragging through deep sand, which continued for miles and was wearisome in the extreme. Our horses plodded along, and the monotony of desert travel was thoroughly established."

Covering only eighteen miles in ten hours, Fannie was more than eager to stop for the night. She quickly realized, however, that she was expected to cook for her family instead of one of the soldiers taking on the task. Coming from a well-to-do family, she had never learned the culinary arts.

A strong wind was blowing, which drove the smoke [from the fire] in my face and eyes. The more I tried to avoid this, the more it seemed to torture me; while my utter lack of knowledge in all culinary matters, especially when prosecuted under such circumstances, was very trying. Baby added to my misery by screaming with pain from her usual attack of colic.

Want of space in our little wagon had compelled us to forego all but the actual necessaries of life; and thus our bill of fare was limited to bacon, hard tack, and a small supply of eggs, which, with coffee, was our only food during that desert travel of five days. I learned to grill bacon and make excellent coffee, but never to enjoy cooking over a camp-fire.

With no tent, the family slept outside under the stars. Every morning, little Mabel usually alerted the camp that dawn had arrived and it was time to move on.

"On reaching Soda Lake [one of the largest alkaline lakes in California] at the end of our seventh day's journey, and second after leaving Camp Cady, we were not a little dismayed to find that the horses were suffering quite severely from the effects of their hard two days' pull through the deep sand. On being unharnessed, one immediately plunged into the lake, and in spite of all efforts remained there. . . . In his heated and exhausted condition he foundered, and to our great sorrow had to be shot."

The company did not to stay long at Soda Lake since it provided no useable water. "During that entire desert journey," Fannie said, "until the Colorado River was reached, we had not a drop of water that could quench thirst. Both men and animals were to be pitied."

Yet even worse conditions lay before them. As they headed east, only stark white plains were visible, unrelieved by even a simple scrub brush. "In all my frontier life and travel," Fannie declared, "I never saw anything so utterly desolate as was that desert."

After nine heat-searing days, the company decided to move only at night as everyone was suffering from the effects of the blistering sun.

We started about sundown on the ninth night, and reaching an old disused house about midnight, prepared to camp. I had been so tortured for several days and nights by the absence of all shelter, that my husband readily complied with the request to place our mattress inside those old walls. The roof had long before disappeared: but it seemed good to be once more in any sort of inclosure [sic], and I lay down very composedly. My sleep was, however, soon disturbed by the strangest sounds. I awakened to find that a veritable carnival was being held by insects, and the uncertainty concerning their species was anything but agreeable. Every imaginable noise could be detected. I bore it silently as long as possible, until confident I heard rattlesnakes, when in great fear I hugged my baby closer, expecting our last moments had come, yet hoping to shield her from their fangs.

Such a night of wretchedness I hope never again to experience. All kinds of horrible sounds terrified me to such an extent that a firm resolve was formed never to pass another night in a place of whose inhabitants I was unaware. I am confident that every sort of vermin infected that old ruined house, and our subsequent perils with visible foes gave me far less anxiety. . . .

Midday again found us on our way; and when we began to descend into the Colorado basin, and caught sight of fort Mojave's adobe walls and the muddy banks of the river, we felt as if the end of a hard journey had at last been reached, and rejoiced exceedingly to see friendly faces and receive a hearty welcome. Knowing that each day's travel was bringing us nearer home, we gladly crossed the river and shook the dust of California from our feet.

Only dallying for two days at the post before starting for Prescott, Fannie was "alarmed at the number of signal fires on all sides, which indicated the near presence of hostile Indians."

As the troops climbed toward higher elevations, she delighted in the new terrain before her: pine trees lined the hillsides of this mountainous region and cooling breezes not felt on the open desert soothed both her and little Mabel. The second day out from Fort Mohave, however, a more grueling route left her exhausted and fearful for her child's safety.

The road had been rough from the start, but nothing to be compared with what we then experienced. After a tedious ascent a long hill was reached, seemingly miles in length, and which must be descended amid boulders strewn all over the road. I was compelled to walk, with baby in my arms, picking my way as best I could from one rock to another. The time occupied in making the descent was three hours. My fatigue can hardly be imagined.

The wagon wheels were lashed together by ropes, which were held by men on either side; and even then the vehicle fairly

bounded onward, each leap almost wrenching it asunder. I
expected every moment to see it lying in ruins. That such was not
its fate was entirely due to the care Mr. Boyd and the men took in
guiding it safely between and over the boulders.

No hill I have ever since seen was like that, and no words
are adequate to give any idea of its horrors. I felt every moment
as if a single mis-step would launch my infant and self into
eternity, and wondered if I could survive the fatigue, even if
successful in placing my feet carefully enough to escape the
greater danger. When finally our little company at the foot of
the hill was reached, I sank, completely exhausted. Many days
passed before I could step without feeling the effects of that ter-
rible scramble in mid-air.

Although she witnessed no Indian uprisings on this journey, Fannie's
fears were enhanced by talk she had heard from other women about
raids on lonely, slow-moving wagon trains.

"My heart was wrung during those travels," she noted, "when, every
hour of the day, we passed a pile of stones that marked a grave. Arizona
seemed to me a very burying-ground—a huge cemetery—for men and
women killed by Indians. . . . I now see that we were then too young
and inexperienced to realize the dangers of our terrible position. It was,
however, soon understood, and before entering the cañon at six o'clock
that evening all warlike preparations possible under the circumstances
had been made."

The cañon was so precipitous on both sides that we seemed to
be traveling between two high walls. The rocks were of that
treacherous gray against which I had been told an Indian could
so effectually conceal himself as to seem but a part of them.
The entire region was weird and awful. The sides of the cañon

towered far above us to almost unseen heights, and as we slowly drove onward, our hearts quivered with excitement and fear at the probability of an attack.

We had proceeded some little distance and were feeling considerably relieved, when suddenly a fearful Indian war-whoop arose. It was so abrupt, and seemed such a natural outcome of our fear's [sic], that only for repeated repetitions I could have believed it imaginary. Others, however, quickly followed, so no doubt could be entertained of their reality. I had only sufficient consciousness to wonder when we should die, and how. I glanced involuntarily at our Chinese servant, who was crouched in one corner of the wagon in a most pitiable heap, and then at our poor little baby, bundled in many wraps and sleeping in her basket. All were silent. No word was uttered, and no sound heard but the lashing of the whip that urged forward our mules. Although they fairly leaped onward, yet we seemed to crawl. Cruel death was momentarily expected.

At last, and it seemed ages, we were out of the cañon and on open ground. Even then no time was lost. The mules were still hurried on. I have often thought that, like Tennyson's brook, we might have "gone on forever" had not a large party of freighters soon been reached, who were camping in front of a blazing wood fire. Their presence gave us that sense of companionship and security so sorely needed. We joined them; and while I sat in the blaze of their fire, Mr. Boyd recounted our perilous ride. The conclusion was reached that we had been spared only because apparently so well prepared to resist attack.

Finally arrived in Prescott, Fannie was delighted by her surroundings, "a most enjoyable climate, never very hot or very cold, but bracing at all seasons."

The Boyds were bivouacked at Fort Whipple, just outside of Prescott. With only three houses on the fort at the time they were allotted a single room in one of the buildings. Each night they had to set up their beds in the living quarters and remove them in the morning.

The day after arriving, Orsemus was ordered to report to Camp Date Creek, about eighty miles up the road, a temporary assignment he was told. Fannie opted to stay at the Prescott post.

"All would have gone well had there been suitable accommodations," she wrote, "but no sooner had Mr. Boyd left than the inspector-general, accompanied by several other officers, arrived, and their baggage was placed in the room I was occupying. There was no alternative but for me to move into the adjoining room, an old, deserted kitchen, which had for years past been the receptacle of miscellaneous *debris*."

My bed had to be made on the floor between two windows, whose panes of glass were either cracked or broken. An old stove, utterly useless, occupied the hearth. As the nights and mornings were very cold I tried to build a fire; but the smoke, instead of ascending, poured into the room in volumes, and compelled me to abandon the task as hopeless. I suffered far more from the cold there than I had while on the march, and longed for a camp-fire.

The kitchen was a perfect curiosity shop. Garments of every imaginable kind, when no longer of use to their owners, had evidently been left there. . . . I counted twenty pairs of boots and shoes, and there were quite as many hats, coats, and nether garments. The corners of that room were to be avoided as one would avoid the plague. My chair, which had been brought from California, was planted in the only clean spot—the floor's immediate center.

Ten days of sleeping in the kitchen were enough for Fannie. When the post surgeon informed her that he was on his way to Camp Date Creek and would be happy to take her and little Mabel along, she jumped at the offer. Unfortunately, while Fannie considered Prescott at least livable if not comfortable, she described Camp Date Creek as "low and malarious."

Although Orsemus was only expecting to be at Camp Date Creek for a short time, his tour of duty lasted almost a year, and for six months, Fannie considered herself the only woman on the post. "It was indeed a desolate and undesirable locality," she said. "The country was ugly, flat, and inexpressibly dreary."

The section stretching in front of our camp was called "bad lands" (mala pice). The only pretty spot at all near was a slow, sluggish stream some miles away, where no one dared remain long for fear of malaria.

Our only associate was the doctor, and subsequently, when a company of infantry arrived, two officers; but for at least six months of that year I was the only woman within at least fifty miles. I found, too, that housekeeping was a burden; for in all the travel from north to south, and the reverse, through Arizona, every one stopped en route. Before we left I felt competent to keep a hotel if experience was any education in the art. Even stage passengers had frequently to be cared for, as in that region it would have been cruel, when delays occurred, to have permitted them to have gone farther without food.

As usual, I had the help of a soldier; but unfortunately one who, when he found that too much was likely to be required of him, took refuge in intoxication; then the entire burden fell upon me. Our little Chinese boy proved a treasure.

Yet despite all its disagreeable amenities, Fannie claimed the year she spent at Camp Date Creek was one of her happiest.

I have often since wondered how it could have been so, for surely no one ever lived more queerly. The houses were built of mud-brick (adobe), which was not, as is usual, plastered either inside or out. Being left unfinished they soon began to crumble in the dry atmosphere, and large holes or openings formed, in which vermin, especially centipeds [sic], found hiding-places. The latter were so plentiful that I have frequently counted a dozen or more crawling in and out of the interstices. Scorpions and rattle-snakes also took up their abode with us, and one snake of a more harmless nature used almost daily to thrust his head through a hole in the floor. Altogether we had plenty of such visitors. . . .

The house consisted of one long room, with a door at either end, and two windows on each side. The room was sufficiently large to enable us to divide it by a canvas curtain, and thus have a sitting-room and bedroom. We felt very happy on account of having a floor other than the ground, though it consisted only of broad, rough, unplanned planks, which had shrunk so that the spaces between them were at least two inches in width, and proved a trap for every little article that fell upon the floor.

The brown, rough adobe walls were very uninviting, and centipeds were so numerous I never dared place our bed within at least two feet of them. The adjoining house, which was vacant, I used for a dining-room. Our kitchen stood as far away in another direction, so I seemed to daily walk miles in the simple routine of housekeeping duties.

She often discovered coyotes hovering at her door and the abundance of rattlesnakes provided her with a hefty collection of rattles for little Mabel.

Mail, due once a week, arrived sporadically and the lack of female companionship sometimes left her melancholy. "I was always delighted when ladies passed through the post," she said, "and invariably begged them to remain as long as possible."

Despite their isolation, the Boyds made the most of their time in central Arizona. On one occasion, they drove to Camp Willow Grove, a temporary post situated along the Hardyville-Prescott Toll Road, built specifically to protect against the Hualapais. The camp was abandoned in October 1869, shortly after the Boyds visited. Their journey to the post, however, was more than Fannie bargained for.

"Everything was delightful when once there," she said, "but we had as usual a disagreeable time going. Two days were consumed on the way. The first night was spent at a stage station where all the strange and uncouth experiences of our Nevada journey were repeated. There was, however, a woman in this rough home who shared her bed with me; but as it was originally intended only for one person, and we each had an infant to care for, it soon became a question of whether or not I, who occupied the side next the wall, should be shoved through it."

In February 1870, Orsemus was ordered to New Mexico. Fannie "had grown to love my Arizona home, if the walls were only rough adobe ones. In just nine months from the time of my arrival at Date Creek, and in mid winter, we left for our new destination. It was the vexation of spirit that I again took up the march."

The trip across the Territory took six weeks with little Mabel just shy of her first birthday.

We journeyed south through Arizona to Tucson, then turned east.
Our outfit consisted of a wall tent, which on encamping at night
was placed on as smooth ground as could be found, and a mess
chest filled with supplies. By placing a support under the raised
cover of the latter, and filling the open space with a board that

fitted nicely, it could be utilized as a table. The interior con-
tained plates and dishes in addition to supplies, and the moment
we reached camp our cook, a soldier, would begin preparations
for a meal, which though ever so plain was always done full jus-
tice to by appetites the long ride had sharpened.

In accordance with my usual habit, I made all necessary
preparations in advance for supplying our wants; and it soon
became more a question of quantity than of quality, for the
generous hearts of Mr. Boyd and the captain always forgot that
our supplies were limited. An instance of their thoughtlessness in
such matters was on one occasion evinced by the arrival, unex-
pectedly to me, of four guests whom they had invited to remain
with us for a few days. To supply food for a week—as it happened
in that case—to those extra people, blessed with unusually good
appetites, taxed my ingenuity.

We had by that time reached the celebrated Indian villages
of the Pimas and Maricopas. [This may have been near Mar-
icopa Wells, about eighty-five miles north of Tucson.] Those two
tribes had been at peace with the pale faces for a century. They
cultivated land, and were industrious and prosperous. Their
villages stretched along the highway for many miles, so we spent
six days among them. They watched our progress in the well-
known, somewhat indifferent Indian fashion, though evincing
real interest when we encamped at night, and swarming about
us with various wares for sale, such as pottery and baskets, both
unique in pattern and very serviceable. The latter were made so
fine in texture and quality as to hold water. The various designs
in which those useful articles were woven displayed much taste.

A few days later, upon arriving in Tucson, Fannie described the Old
Pueblo as "an insignificant town of flat mud houses so unprepossessing

that we were glad to drive through without stopping, and encamp beside a beautiful stream two miles beyond."

Finally finding a church in Arizona Territory, she was in awe of Mission San Xavier del Bac just south of Tucson.

I cannot express the astonishment excited by the sight of that house of worship built in those vast wilds, hundreds of miles from all civilization. The edifice, of noble proportions, was of red brick and whitish stucco. Both belfry and tower were complete. The interior decorations were profuse, and covered the walls. The floor, once hard and smooth, had been worn into hollows by the footsteps of countless devotees, whose race even was unknown, though surmised to be that of the ancient Aztecs, or followers of Montezuma.

I doubt if even in Europe, with its mystic shrines dating back countless ages, I could have experienced a more profound sense of awe than when standing in that absolutely desert spot, and realizing that skilled hands had once erected there such a monument.

In that old church were marriage records dating back hundreds of years; but the structure was to me the all absorbing wonder.

The followers of Montezuma had nothing to do with building San Xavier Church, but it does date back to 1692, when Father Eusebio Kino founded a Catholic mission at the site. In 1783, Franciscan missionary Father Juan Bautista Velderrain began construction on the present structure using Tohono O'odham people to build the church. With the Gadsden Purchase of 1854, the mission lay on land purchased by the United States. The old basilica was certainly a mirage in the desert for a New York City girl like Fannie.

Once again on the road, the procession moved quickly through Apache territory, stopping for only a few days at Camp Bowie. Troops there had been involved as recently as the prior year in a skirmish with the Chiricahua Apache warrior Cochise. "A large guard was always detailed to watch the outposts," Fannie noted, "and yet so subtle, as is well known, are Indians, that although close at hand they were seldom caught."

That strange little fort in the very heart of the mountain fastness sheltered a number of women and children. As usual, we received a hearty welcome, and were feasted and fêted in true army fashion. The post surgeon vacated his room in our honor; for which we were very grateful, especially when one of those terrible mountain blizzards came on, in which clouds of dust so thick are formed that objects cannot be distinguished at a distance of ten feet. The room we occupied was built of logs, and dust blew through the crevices until it seemed as if we were a part of the universal grit. The tents were simply uninhabitable, though before our destination was reached we were compelled to occupy them through what seemed fully as severe a storm.

Finally arriving at New Mexico's Fort Stanton, Fannie was relieved her travels were at an end, at least for a while. Orsemus continued his service in the military until his untimely death in 1885 while stationed, once again, in New Mexico. He was only forty-one years old.

Fannie had continued to care for her husband throughout his military career. She also gave birth to two more children: James William was born in 1871 while the family was back in New York, and Henry followed in 1877 during a stint in Texas.

Thirty-seven years old when her husband died, Fannie petitioned the military for an allowance and received the standard widow's pension of twenty dollars per month.

She initially settled in Washington, DC, and later moved to New York, but wanderlust had taken a strong hold on Fannie during her days of traipsing from one Army post to another, and through her remaining years she traveled extensively. Around 1908 she bought a house in New Jersey and died there on May 2, 1926, at the age of seventy-eight.

Fannie embraced and enjoyed many of her travels along western trails, but it was her love for her husband that kept her steadfast and uncomplaining through those trying days. She grew to enjoy the West and soon found herself longing to return to the wilds of desert living instead of the city life of which she thought so highly before her excursion into Arizona.

"I shall never become reconciled to localities where the eye cannot look for miles and miles beyond the spot where one stands," she wrote, "and where the density of the atmosphere circumscribes the view, limiting it to a comparatively short distance. I have traveled in New Mexico and Arizona for days, when on starting early in the morning the objective point of my journey, and an endless stretch of road, perhaps for a hundred miles, could be seen.

"To mount a horse, such as can be found only in the West, perfect for the purpose, and gallop over prairies, completely losing one's self in vast and illimitable space, as silent as lonely, is to leave every petty care, and feel the contented frame of mind which can only be produced by such surroundings. In those grand wastes one is truly alone with God. Oh, I love the West, and dislike to think that the day will surely come when it will teem with human life and all its warring elements!"

CHAPTER 5

The Authority of a Riding Whip

Sarah Elvira Camp Upham

Once Sarah "Sally" Camp decided to marry First Lieutenant Frank Kidder Upham on April 1, 1871, she never looked back on what her life might have been had she chosen differently. Frank was a career Army man serving during the Civil War and already a veteran of western military posts.

Sarah left no record of her time in Arizona, or at any of the posts where her husband was stationed during their twenty-eight-year marriage. Yet Frank thought so highly of his wife's intelligence and bravery that he lauded her in an article about their two-year stint at Camp Apache, giving Sarah credit for keeping the peace on at least one occasion. Frank's tribute to his wife, "Incidents of Regular Army Life in Time of Peace," which was published in the *Overland Monthly* in 1885, confirms how many soldiers stationed in the West understood and recognized the sacrifices made by families during their time on the western frontier. Frank also included a vivid portrayal of housing conditions and post life during the couple's residency at Camp Apache.

Sarah was born on November 23, 1852, in Fillmore, Illinois, just south of Springfield. She was still a child when the family moved 200 miles north to Dixon. At age eighteen she married First Lieutenant Frank Upham who, at the time, was stationed in San Francisco.

The couple spent their honeymoon traveling the Pacific Railroad from Illinois to California. Frank had recently served in Arizona Territory and hoped his next assignment would be in more agreeable surroundings such as the Oregon or Washington Territories. Unfortunately, he was ordered to return to the dust and heat of Arizona, this time to Camp Apache.

That June, the couple boarded a steamer out of San Francisco for San Diego and made their way across the desert in an Army ambulance. The trip took six weeks during the hottest part of the Arizona summer. Out of Tucson, they were accompanied "with an escort of twenty mounted men," Frank wrote,

riding near our wagons, and constantly on the lookout for hostile Indians; a regular guard was mounted at night, as a necessary precaution against the surprise of our camp by the murderous savages who infested the country bordering upon the San Pedro River and Dragoon Mountains, and of whose bloody work we were daily reminded by the lonely graves at the roadside. These were, in most instances, marked with a rude cross, probably placed there by the friendly hands of those who had known the victims in life, or possibly by the passing stranger, who knew not how soon he too might be in need of the same kindly office.

This was nearly fifteen years ago; and now, when I hear others carelessly mention a trip by rail to the same locality and return as a journey of a few days, or a week at most, a momentary feeling akin to envy or anger comes over me; and it is difficult to realize that it has been possible for even steam and the locomotive to accomplish such results—to have apparently annihilated the absolute waste and desolation through which we passed so wearily.

An end came, however, as it always does, and the journey itself is at this distance recalled with even pleasant recollections of the brighter incidents connected with it: for, thanks to that peculiar characteristic of the human mind which enables us to forget all but the brighter spots, those alone have been mainly remembered.

The long-looked-for station [Camp Apache], which was finally reached, and which, for a time, ended our ambulance and tent life, was then called a camp, though it has since attained to the more dignified title of a fort [Camp Apache became a fort in 1879]; having been, in the mean time, however, entirely rebuilt, after the manner of modern garrisons. But at that time nearly all frontier stations were known as camps; as in fact they should have been, for they were not more than the name implied.

This station consisted of a lot of rough log buildings, which had been constructed by soldier labor, and accordingly in the most primitive manner. They were begun a few months before our arrival—when the post had first been located and established— and were still but partially completed. The whole was arranged in the form of a camp of cavalry, and was originally laid out with the same military precision, in strict accordance with the plan found in the army regulations. So many outside structures in the way of stables, quartermaster's corrals, a sutler's store, and so forth, besides numerous Indian rancherias, had, however, been permitted or caused to spring up in the immediate vicinity—all of which were out of uniformity with the original plans—that upon approaching the post by the road from Tucson, as we did, it had more the appearance of a frontier town or mining camp, quietly resting on a ridge or knoll which crossed the narrow valley, than of a military post, garrisoned by two troops of cavalry and two companies of infantry belonging to the regular army of the United States. But notwithstanding the want of that regularity in appearance which one might have expected to meet, it was not destitute of a certain natural attractiveness, or even beauty, owning to its picturesque environment especially.

The journey had been a tiresome one, and for more than two hundred miles no sign of human life or habitation had been visible; consequently, the satisfaction with which we reached our destination may be understood.

As we entered the post, the line of officers' quarters extended for a quarter of a mile parallel to a cañon one hundred yards in the rear. The walls of this cañon were nearly, if not quite, perpendicular, and through it fifty or sixty yards below ran a beautiful mountain stream, whose source was in the distance snow-capped peaks visible against the horizon to the eastward.

The officers' quarters faced those of the soldiers, which consisted of six log cabins to each company, running at right angles to the officers' line, about eighty yards from it; the intervening space formed a parade ground.

The view from both front and rear of the post, though attractive, was limited, and consisted principally of the immediate, and rather abrupt, pine and juniper covered mountain sides. To the east and west, up and down the valley, it was more extended, though also confined to mountain scenery, but of such a grand description that the eye never tired of resting upon it: made up of ridges, crags, and distant peaks, blending with the sky in wild, fantastic shapes. At sunset the landscape was tinted with gorgeous prismatic effects, seldom equaled anywhere.

The quarters of the officers varied but little, if at all, in their appearance, manner of construction, or dimensions. All were equally bad, and such as at the present time even the army on the frontier would object to, and consider unfit for habitation. Those that we went into were a sample of others; a building eighteen by twenty feet, the chinks between the logs daubed with adobe mud, both inside and out; the interior, one room, a rough, unplaned [sic] board floor, a large fire-place at one end—the chimney on the outside—at the other a door, the only entrance or exit, with a window on one side of the room, consisting of a single sash with six lights of glass, swinging inward on its hinges. No ceiling whatever, but the bare rafters covered with rough boards formed an unshingled roof overhead, which, though affording excellent ventilation, was no protection from the weather, the boards having become so warped and twisted by the sun as to admit of frequent streaks of both sunlight and moonlight, and thus partially compensate for the want of more windows.

In this cabin we were soon domiciled, for it was the work of but a few hours to put down the carpet and arrange the few simple articles of furniture which had been brought with us from San Francisco, or had been manufactured by the post quartermaster; and while the weather continued pleasant, we thought we were very comfortable—as much so as our neighbors, at least, which is always a satisfactory feeling.

But in September, when the terrible rain and thunder storms came, it was quite a different matter, and we were obliged to go into camp inside the house. This was done by nailing a piece of canvas to the logs on the side of the room, about ten feet from the floor, and stretching the opposite side over a pole supported by two uprights, by this means improvising a shelter after the fashion of a tent, under which it was possible to keep dry until the storm passed. Such articles as we were unable to move under this shelter were also covered with canvas, so far as practicable. Fortunately, the rains, though frequent at this season, were of short duration; but they came down in torrents while they lasted. The novelty of the situation was, however, something; and it did not then seem so bad as it does now in recalling it.

In our single apartment we lived, slept, and ate our meals, though the cooking was done in a smaller building of the same character which belonged to this establishment, about twenty feet distant, directly in the rear. The one room of this was alike

the kitchen and a general store room (the cook slept in a tent).
Here the meals were prepared, and they were brought hence by
"our man," on a tray, into the "large house," where the board
was spread—a cow bell which I had borrowed from the quarter-
master's store-house proving to be a satisfactory substitute for the
regular call bell with which we had forgotten to provide ourselves
while fitting out before leaving San Francisco.

As will be readily inferred, our daily domestic life was a
quiet and simple one. Society at first consisted of the invalid wife
of our married officer, who rarely left her room, and who had,
before our arrival, been without female society for more than
a year. She was only waiting to gain strength enough to enable
her to reach her home in Philadelphia, whither she started a few
weeks later.

Besides this lady and her husband, there were a few bachelor
officers. We came in contact with no others socially, and during
the two years passed at this station my wife had no society of
her own sex, with the exception of a short period—about six
months—during which the wives of two other officers were with
them; so that we were mainly dependent upon ourselves for
society. During the pleasant portions of the year we took occa-
sional trips, sometimes on horseback or in the ambulance, but
more frequently on foot, among the hills and pine trees, or along
the river, occasionally looking in on some of the Indian camps,
where we were always welcome, and where a white lady was an
object of singular curiosity.

Points and objects of interest were not wanting in a locality
for which nature had done so much, and we were seldom at a loss
where to go, when my occupations admitted of going at all.

But of all the surrounding country the most attractive stroll
was through the narrow cañon in the rear of the post, from the

entrance to the end of which was about a mile, and through which an abandoned Indian trail was discovered. This the soldiers had made passable by cutting away a portion of the almost tropical growth of tangled vines and bushes which had accumulated and obstructed the trail, and felling trees to serve as bridges on which to cross the little stream.

The stream abounded in miniature cascades, and was filled with trout. Nearly the entire distance was shut in by steep walls on either side; to many of its depths the sun daily penetrated but an hour or two, and during the hottest of summer days one could always be sure of a cool and shady retreat here.

Until the recesses of this cañon had been thoroughly explored, it had not been deemed prudent to enter it, unless armed and prepared for an encounter with the bears which were supposed to frequent, if not to inhabit it. This impression originated in the fact that one evening at sunset, shortly after our arrival, a large black bear was seen to emerge from the mouth of the cañon at a point above the post, and trot deliberately and directly along, passing the open ground in rear of the officers' kitchens, between them and the edge of the cañon.

It so happened that I was the first to observe his approach, and had time enough to enable me to go into my quarters, get a carbine—which was always kept between the mattresses of the bed, loaded and in readiness for immediate use—and wait for the bear, who was to pass within fifty yards of the house.

I had never killed a bear, but was anxious to do so—perhaps too anxious, or possibly the opportunity was too good. At all events, I placed myself behind the corner of the kitchen, and waited until I could almost see his eyes, then fired; but to my surprise and mortification—for I had always considered myself a fair shot with a rifle—he only wiggled his stumpy tail a little, *and shambled on down the line in his lumbering but singularly rapid gait.*

By this time others had also comprehended the situation, and were lying in wait for him in the same manner, though their opportunities were not quite equal to mine; but although at least forty bullets were sent after him from the cavalry carbines and infantry "long toms" by both officers and soldiers, Bruin escaped.

In doing this he was obliged to run the gauntlet of nearly the entire line, until coming to a point on the edge of the cliff which was a trifle less precipitous than the rest, he descended with the agility of a cat, and was up the wall of the opposite side of the cañon as quickly, though the firing continued at long range until he was lost to sight among the junipers. No doubt he carried lead with him, but evidently not enough to make him our "meat"; and he possibly laughed in his sleeve, as he trotted away, at the ridiculous marksmanship of the "brutal soldiery."

Diligent search through all parts of the cañon after this failed to discover any bear sign, however, and there ceased to be further apprehension about entering it.

Serving as post quartermaster and commissary, Frank was seldom home during the day as his duties consisted of dealing with about 1,400 Apaches coming onto the post to be counted and to obtain rations. Sarah had to find her own amusements.

"Books and other literature were not wanting," Frank noted, "as an abundant supply of magazines and newspapers reached the post."

But one can not read constantly, and among other expedients she [Sarah] began to acquire a knowledge of the Indian, or more especially of the Apache language; and very frequently on pleas-

ant mornings, after domestic affairs had received the necessary attention, and the simple housekeeping was arranged for the day, a few of the most intelligent young Indians of both sexes would collect outside the little window of our house, where from the inside she would hold protracted interviews with them— communicating at first through the medium of signs, or of a few Spanish words which the Indians had pick up. But presently this intercourse was conducted entirely by means of the Indian tongue, with which she rapidly became conversant, to the manifest surprise and delight of the Indians themselves. In this manner, she, in a few months, acquired a more extensive knowledge of the Apache language than any white person who was connected with the post at that time.

She did not meet with the same degree of success, however, in her attempts to teach the young Indian idea how to shoot [write]; and though she labored faithfully with several of the most promising, she only got so far with "Phillipi," who was the brightest, (and had acquired his Spanish name by a short captivity among the Mexicans when very young), that he was able to print in large ungainly capitals on the slate, the words, "My sore face"—after which exploit even he, apparently, decided that he had sufficiently penetrated the depths of English literature, and ceased to apply himself further.

The knowledge thus acquired gave her an established reputation with the various bands on the reservation, where, as with white people, nothing was lost by being repeated—and Indians are notorious gossips among themselves. The chiefs and head men made regular calls at the house, at proper intervals, and seemed by common consent to concede to her a status which was unusual for a woman, and to which one of their own race could never have hoped to attain.

Doubtless, had she been so inclined, she might have exerted a strong influence in their affairs, but she was without ambition in that direction. A more practical result of this knowledge was realized in the fact that we were pretty regularly supplied with game of various kinds at a low price—fine wild turkeys, when in season, weighing from twelve to fifteen pounds, for ten pounds of flour; the latter purchased from the post commissary at three cents per pound. This was, however, only practicable during the summer months. The winter was lonesome and dreary, though fortunately of short duration and not severe.

Mail facilities were uncertain and irregular, and frequently during the winter there was no mail for three or four weeks at a time. Once we were five weeks without a mail, though one finally made its appearance, quite unexpectedly, by the way of New Mexico, on the top of a load of freight; and after this we considered ourselves greatly favored by a weekly mail from Santa Fé, letters from friends in the East reaching us in ten or twelve days.

On September 7, 1872, Sarah gave birth to son Frank Brooks Upham at Camp Apache. She had three more children over the ensuing years. John Southworth Upham was born on November 5, 1881, while the family was stationed at Fort Walla Walla, Washington; followed by Ethelbertha Upham on February 8, 1883, in San Francisco. The youngest, Edith Upham, arrived at Fort Walla Walla on May 17, 1884.

According to Frank, "During the second year [at Camp Apache] the Indians became more and more troublesome and harder to control . . . so much so, that it became advisable to exclude them from the limits of the post by the necessary guard, and my wife accordingly saw but little of them, only those visiting our house who had a special permit for that purpose, and this confined to a few of the more important personages."

One afternoon an unusual commotion was suddenly observed among some of them, who had collected at a point near the Tucson road to the eastward of the post, and before it was realized, or any steps could possibly have been taken by the guard to prevent it, a number of Indians fled rapidly in the direction of the post, closely pursued by others, in a state of partial drunkenness, hallooing and shooting with guns, and bows and arrows, as they closely followed behind.

[O]ur house was the first and most exposed in this direction, and here the fugitives immediately came, taking refuge in the rear of the house, and about it, and behind the big chimney which ran up to the outside; either hoping to obtain protection, or for the purpose of making a stand, as they were also armed.

The situation in the inside of the house was critical and alarming: as usual at that time of day, I was absent. My wife and child were alone, and she fully understood the situation. The man who should have been in the kitchen—he was there but a few minutes previously—or somewhere within call, was nowhere to be seen, and had undoubtedly run away ingloriously or hidden when he saw the Indians coming, though he had served during the whole war of the rebellion as an enlisted man, and was at one time a sergeant.

Immediate action was necessary, for the danger from a chance bullet coming through the chinks in the logs was considerable, and not to be despised; besides which, the possibility of the Indians crowding their way inside the house, when they found she [Sarah] was alone, was not pleasant to contemplate.

She did not long remain undecided, however, but took a small riding whip which hung against the wall, went at once outside the house, and drove them away by a lively application of the little whip to their bare feet and ankles. Several of these intruders were young Indians with whom she had a personal acquaintance; but they all immediately sneaked off with a sickly smile, and would, no doubt, have greatly preferred to have faced the fire of the other party, to be subjected to the mortification and disgrace of being thus dealt with by a woman.

The whole incident occurred in a very short time; and by the time the guard reached the ground, the cause of the alarm was over and the Indians gone. I only learned of its occurrence several hours later, at dinner-time.

Hence Sarah left her mark, in more than one way, during her time at Camp Apache.

In 1872, with their tour of duty over, the family headed to Santa Fe, where Frank put his wife and child on an eastward-bound train. His company set off in the opposite direction to fight in the 1872–1873 Modoc War in the northern part of California and southern Oregon.

In 1882, Frank was promoted to captain. He retired in 1892 and became quartermaster and treasurer of the National Home for Disabled Volunteer Soldiers in Los Angeles.

One of Frank's duties was to transfer the monthly payroll from the railroad station to the soldiers' home. On October 17, 1899, Frank was notified that the payroll had arrived at the depot. Retrieving a revolver from his desk to arm himself while carrying such a large amount of money, he started toward the door. The gun caught on the edge of the table and fired, the bullet hitting Frank in the head, killing him instantly. Frank Upham is buried in Los Angeles.

Sarah received the usual widow's pension of twenty dollars a month. She eventually returned to Dixon, Illinois, and became active in social organizations including the Phidian Art Club that promoted art, literature, and music.

Sarah died in Canandaigua, New York, in 1921 at the age of sixty-nine. She was brought back to Los Angeles and is buried beside her husband.

Although Sarah left no words of her own describing her time at Fort Apache, her husband acknowledged she had probably saved the post from a disastrous incident because of her friendly association with the Apache people. He was insistent that her deeds be recorded and remembered.

PART III

———•●•———

THE FAMILY

Not only did women bring west all the furnishings they could cram into their weight allotment, absolute necessities such as tableware, bedding, and enough clothing to last them for months, they also added items such as delicate chinaware and family heirlooms that sometimes failed to make it over treacherous mountain ranges. Martha Summerhayes lost all her kitchenware and fine china when the buckboard carrying her precious goods careened down a mountainside. At the time, she mourned the loss of her prized belongings but soon realized there were more important concerns to be tended to and cared for beyond pots and pans.

The children who came west with their families often thrived in the openness of the land, the fresh air, and outdoor activities they would not have enjoyed back east in crowded cities and cloistered households. The journey itself thrilled many youngsters as they rode across the open range, climbed rugged mountains, and forded unnavigated waterways. They mingled freely with other children and did not concern themselves with social rankings. They invented their own games, learned to fish and hunt, and sometimes found themselves free from schooling, a situation that undoubtedly concerned their parents.

Children did suffer from illness and exposure to strange new plants and animals. Diseases spread rapidly through unsanitary Army posts, claiming the young and susceptible. Measles, diphtheria, dysentery, scurvy, and cholera were just a few of the afflictions that permeated most early forts. When Ellen Biddle's son got into a patch of poisoned oak, the rash covered his entire body. Alice Grierson, whose husband,

Military families at Fort McDowell circa 1885 AZ State Library, Archives, and Public Records, History and Archives Division, Phoenix, #97-3510

Colonel Benjamin Harrison Grierson, was stationed at Fort Whipple and later at Fort Grant, from 1885 to 1886, suffered the loss of her daughter from what was probably typhoid fever.

Few schools existed on military posts until 1866, when the Army authorized a building be dedicated as a schoolhouse. By 1881, educational guidelines were in place at most post schools with soldiers selected to teach youngsters for the extra pay of thirty-five cents a day. Fort Bowie initiated a school in 1879 for both officers and enlisted men's children, with evening classes held for soldiers who wished to further their educations. Unfortunately, the school only lasted two years.

Frequently, officers' children were sent back east to live with extended family members while furthering their educations in more traditional schools. Ellen Biddle agonized over leaving her two boys at a boarding school in Connecticut before heading to Arizona with her young daughter. When her next two youngsters were ready for school, she decided not to go with her husband but remained back east rather than be separated from her children.

Military families faced challenging decisions when it came to their children; one of the most concerning was deciding what plans to make when the wife was about to give birth on an isolated outpost with the possibility of no doctor in attendance.

Expectant women considered themselves lucky if a post surgeon was on hand to assist during their pregnancy, although many of them felt these men ill equipped to handle a delivery. Enlisted men's wives and laundresses frequently served as midwives since they often had more experience than the post doctor.

Women accepted they might not survive if complications occurred before, during, or after delivery, and that their infant stood even less chance if the birth was not handled properly. At Fort Whipple in 1877, both Ellen Biddle and Fannie Kautz, the commanding officer's wife, lost newborns within days of each other even though there was a doctor in attendance. Evy Alexander gave birth to five children throughout her years traveling with the military and outlived every one of them.

Women who were separated from their husbands for long periods knew they ran the risk of becoming pregnant as soon as they reunited. After a long absence from her husband, Alice Grierson wrote to him in 1871, "There is no use in planning for another trip for me, in all probability after I have been with you a few months I shall be in no condition for traveling, if it can possibly be avoided. . . . Both of us will know one thing, which will inevitably occur, if the good Lord permits us to meet again, and are both well aware of the *possible* consequences which may follow." Alice gave birth to seven children during the course of her marriage.

Maintaining a healthy and well-nourished family were primary concerns for military wives. Families relied on whatever was available in the post commissary for sustenance. Meat was usually plentiful on most western posts, with hunting an enjoyable pastime for both women and men, although fresh fruits and vegetables were almost nonexistent. Even if these items could be purchased in a nearby town, or at the sutler's store, the cost was almost prohibitive. In Arizona, flour could be obtained from Sonora, Mexico, although it was gritty and unpalatable. And if soldiers could be coerced into roping wild cattle and milking them, fresh milk was enjoyed around the breakfast table.

Soldiers often started their own small gardens, and women soon found this to be a pleasurable as well as advantageous pastime that provided fresh produce for their families. Melons, beans, corn, and a variety of greens could be grown depending on the location of the post.

While it may appear that the military mostly existed on hardtack, coffee, and canned goods, this was not the case among officers who were obliged to entertain and serve appetizing and elaborate meals to visiting officials. Meats and seafood appeared on their tables, brought in from the West Coast buried in costly ice. One might see lobster served by the commanding officer's wife along with bountiful salads and decadent desserts. After a sumptuous repast, the men adjourned to enjoy cigars that had been shipped all the way from New York.

Military wives were expected to plan these extravagant and decorative meals but they certainly did not do the cooking. Officers' wives usually employed at least one if not more servants. Some brought their maids and cooks with them while others relied on enlisted men or their wives to produce whatever the menu demanded.

Fashion added another layer to a woman's social status, with many relying on their eastern relatives to send reports on the latest trends in

Officers and wives picnicking at Fort Grant circa 1876 Arizona Historical Society, Places-Ft. Grant Photo File, #45297

both clothing and hairstyles. They ordered the latest dresses and hats only to wait months for delivery. A new outfit on a western post might be out of date by the time it arrived but still generate envy among the female ranks.

Summers were particularly hard on women stationed on southern Arizona posts and left many wilting in the high temperatures and blazing sun since their clothing did not adapt well to the heat and humidity that permeated desert wastelands. A woman's wardrobe usually consisted of a chemise and corset, a pair of drawers, petticoats (usually more than one), stockings, garters, and shoes, all beneath a dress that had long sleeves and a high neckline. Bustles and steel hoops were added if the occasion called for more elaborate attire.

Ironically, while women continued to dress in the Victorian style of almost complete coverup, if a dance or hop was held at a post, ball gowns usually exposed bare arms and scantily covered bosoms.

While at Fort McDowell, Evy Alexander complained that the "intense heat of summer makes it a hazardous place for a teething child." But once fall came, she was delighted that she and her baby could spend most of their time outdoors.

At Fort Grant, in the southeastern part of the territory, Fanny Corbusier learned to hang her water jugs in the shade to keep the liquid somewhat cool. One Fourth of July, her husband sent to Los Angeles for one hundred pounds of ice with the idea of making ice cream. It arrived packed in sawdust but unfortunately, only five pounds of ice survived the trip, enough for a pitcher of cool water.

Elizabeth Burt relished the blocks of ice that were delivered to the post occasionally, making meals a little more palatable. "Four days of each week were thus enjoyed," she said, "but in the other three, as far as the table was concerned, the butter was oil, the cheese already melted for a rarebit; the quail of which the hunters brought in great numbers, were delicious on ice days but at other times had to be eaten as soon as killed."

For centuries, women all over the world have been making homes for their families under extraordinary circumstances. They adapt to whatever conditions and situations they face and will do almost anything to protect their families.

On the early western frontier, the journals, diaries, and letters of such women contain vivid accounts of their experiences coping with the loss of and separation from their children, managing with whatever was available to sustain their families, and maintaining the social status necessary for their husbands to rise in rank.

* * *

Two women whose experiences in Arizona Territory varied significantly left detailed accounts of their families' good times and the sometimes horrific events they encountered.

Ellen Biddle enjoyed the social life that was prevalent at Prescott's Fort Whipple before heading south to Fort Grant. Her time in the territory is noteworthy since Ellen was considered to be in fragile health most of her life, yet she endured countless hardships and rose to each occasion as an indomitable heroine ready to defend her family with remarkable physical as well as emotional strength. She lost an infant while at Whipple and later lost another child. Separated from her other children during the years she left them back east for their educations, her experiences typify what many women endured coming west with their husbands.

Katharine Cochran's memoirs describe an Indian uprising that occurred during her time at Fort Apache. The Battle at Cibecue Creek has been written of and discussed by numerous historians. Katharine presents a graphic picture of the event from a woman's perspective, detailing how she protected her children from flying bullets while waiting to see if her husband would return dead or alive.

CHAPTER 6

Cacti in Bloom—Red, Purple, Yellow, and White

Ellen McGowan Biddle

Ellen Biddle was not a physically strong woman, and her frail constitution sometimes forced her to remain behind as her husband's military career took him across the country. When it came to the care of her children, however, Ellen demonstrated the strength and tenacity women have exhibited since time began. If her children were in danger, Ellen reacted with boldness and ferocity. And if she had to leave her children in order for them to obtain a decent education, she bravely bade them farewell, never shedding a tear until beyond their sight.

Born in New Jersey on June 13, 1841, Ellen McGowan was well aware what was expected of a military wife since her father, Captain John McGowan, had honorably served with the United States Navy. When she married James Biddle on November 20, 1862, he was already a captain with the Fifteenth United States Infantry and would continue his military career throughout the Civil War and on the western frontier.

Ellen wrote about her time traveling with military troops in her book *Reminiscences of a Soldier's Wife*, which was published in 1907. A gifted writer, Ellen chronicled her years on Army posts and explicitly portrayed the trials and tribulations that many military wives experienced. Her time in Arizona is particularly fascinating and captivating.

The Biddle marriage was fruitful: Ellen bore seven children although not all survived. John "Jack" McGowan Biddle was born in New Jersey in 1865, followed by David Harmony Biddle in 1867. Both boys were the delight of their mother.

After the Civil War, the Biddles' first tour of western duty took them to Texas and Ellen discovered a strength she was unaware she possessed, but that often comes to parents when their children are at risk.

Ellen McGowan Biddle

Biddle, Ellen McGowan.
*Reminiscences of a Soldier's
Wife.* Philadelphia: J. B.
Lippincott Company, 1907.

She and the boys enjoyed rides into the country to relieve the tedium of post life on the barren Texas plain. One afternoon, a new driver was assigned to her coach and Ellen quickly assessed the man was so drunk he almost fell off the carriage. "As soon as I realized our danger," she wrote, "I told the boys to lie flat on the bottom of the carriage, and notwithstanding the horses were now running, I succeeded in climbing through the window into the seat next [to] the driver and took the reins from him."

Although I could not stop the horses at once I guided them; fortunately the road was broad, and there were but few teams on it. No one came to our rescue, but after the horses had run some distance we came to a cross road, into which I turned them, thinking it would take us nearer home, which it did. Gradually the horses stopped running; poor things, they were not vicious, only frightened and excited from the man pulling them. As soon as they heard my voice they quieted down but trembled all over with fear.

When we got in sight of our cottage I saw the Colonel [husband James] on the sidewalk talking with Captain Whitney. I drove up to the house and he took in the situation at once and took the horses' heads; I remember no more about it for I had fainted, the relief being so great. Colonel carried me into the house, while the boys jumped from the bottom of the carriage and told what had happened. Captain Whitney took the horses to the stable to see that they had proper treatment, while the driver was sent to the guard-house to sober up and reap the consequences. I often wondered where I got the strength to guide the horses as I did.

After leaving Texas, Ellen and the boys spent time in Philadelphia while Ellen awaited the birth of her third child, Ellen McGowan "Nellie" Biddle, in 1869.

When her husband was ordered to Camp Halleck, Nevada, she and the children went with him. She delivered a stillborn child while there.

In 1875, James was appointed acting assistant inspector general of the Department of Arizona, a position he maintained until late 1880. He was ordered to report to Fort Whipple just outside of Prescott. Ellen, having endured posts in Texas and Nevada, as well as watching her husband take five-year-old David with him onto the battlefield during the 1872 Modoc War, had to choose between going with her husband or returning east with her children. She was not at all pleased with this new post in the wilds of Arizona as she had heard stories that ran rampant through military families of Indians taking women and children captive. These rumors brought fear and dread to women headed into hostile territory.

Jack and David were now school age, and with few educational facilities in Arizona, she had a difficult choice to make, but finally put the boys in a Connecticut school and set off to join her husband in Arizona with little Nellie in tow.

"I folded each one to my heart," she said as she left her sons, "and kissed them again and again, knowing I was going a long distance from them, but never dreaming so many years would pass before I would see them again. I looked back at them as I drove away. The two stood side by side, holding each other's hand. I burst into a flood of tears and wept as I had never wept before in my life."

In January 1876, Ellen boarded a train with Nellie and a nurse that would take them through Chicago, Omaha, and Ogden before reaching their destination of San Francisco. Between Ogden and their final stop, heavy snow on the tracks delayed the train for three days.

Finally arriving in San Francisco, they stayed through the winter before starting for Arizona. By April the family was on the ship *Newbern* heading down the coast toward the Colorado River, the same boat Martha Summerhayes had taken to Ehrenberg just a few years before.

The Colorado Steam Navigation Company was the only business that ran steamers along the banks of the Colorado River between Arizona Territory and California. Every twenty days, a vessel left San Francisco destined for the Gulf of California, a distance of 1,900 miles, on a journey that usually took about two weeks. From the gulf, passengers were put on river boats that carried them 175 miles up the Colorado River to Fort Yuma, another five-day passage. Transferred again, ferries chugged on upriver to destinations along the coastline.

"At the mouth of the Colorado River we were transferred in small rowboats to a small steamer, called 'The Cocopah,' commanded by Captain [Isaac] Polhemus," Ellen wrote.

The boat to which we were transferred was a broad, low, flat, stern-wheeler, with an upper deck without a railing around it; the officers and their families and any civilians who might be going to the Territory occupied this part of the boat; soldiers and Chinamen were below.

The Colorado, broad, shallow and full of quicksands that are constantly changing, is a remarkable river; it flows through deep cañons in Nevada, the walls of which in some places rise over six thousand feet; it also flows through the Great Cañon [Grand Canyon], and then through broad, sluggish channels to the sea; the only navigation is along that part of the country where the river separates California and Arizona where we were travelling, the whole country being barren and barbarous. A Cocopah Indian stood at the bow of the boat with a long pole measuring the depth of the water, calling every few moments in measured, monotonous tones its depth, and when it would get too low for the wheels to revolve two men would jump overboard carrying a long heavy chain; they would often go far out of sight, and fastening these chains into rings that were made fast in the rocks, they would wind the boat up to the rings; the chains would be taken off and we would go on.

Twelve days later, the steamer arrived at Fort Yuma.

"After our boat was unloaded," Ellen recalled, "which took five days, and our cargo put on a smaller boat, we again started up the river."

Although it was a monotonous journey, Ellen seemed to enjoy the novelty of the excursion aboard the small, cramped craft.

We had a large coop on the deck filled with ducks. In some way a number of them got out and flew overboard. The boat was stopped, two small boats were lowered, and some men went after them. As the men would get near enough to touch them the ducks would dive down, out of sight, and come up at some distance away. It was great fun for us watching, and the soldiers and

Chinamen had a good many bets on them. We lost three or four of the ducks, and it was a serious loss in that part of the land, as I afterwards found out.

We reached Ehrenberg just before sundown four days after leaving Fort Yuma. It was only a depot for supplies that were shipped to the forts in all parts of the Territory; and here, entirely isolated from the world, lived Lieutenant and Mrs. Jack [Martha] Summerhays [sic], with only one other white man—a Mr. Vandevere, the clerk or secretary. They were very glad to see us and gave us the warmest welcome, though we had never before met.

We had a very good dinner, notwithstanding it was so far out of the world, for most army women learned to cook and make the best of everything that came within reach. I was somewhat surprised when a very tall, thin Indian came in the dining-room to serve the dinner, which he did quite well.

There was much to talk about before I thought of putting my little one to bed, and I asked Mrs. Summerhays if I might have a tub of warm water to give Nelly a bath [Ellen sometimes wrote her daughter's name as "Nelly," other times "Nellie"]. In a little while she told me it was ready in my room (which I soon learned was her own she had given up to me). We said good-night, and going to the room I undressed the child and gave her a refreshing bath, the first that she had had since leaving San Francisco. She soon fell asleep and after I had straightened the room a bit, I decided I would get in the tub. I had just sat down in the water when my room door was silently opened and in walked the tall Indian carrying a tray filled with silver before him. I scarcely breathed so great was my fright. He walked over to the table, put the tray down, and as silently walked out, looking neither to the right or the left. It is useless for me to attempt to describe what I felt, it would convey nothing.

Ellen and Martha Summerhayes probably discussed the long trip from San Francisco on the steamship *Newbern* as well as the hot, uncomfortable ride up the Colorado River on the *Cocopah*, vessels Martha had also taken, although no ducks escaped during her journey.

Martha was not as distressed with half-naked Natives as was Ellen. She described her servant Charley who interrupted Ellen's bath as appealing "to my aesthetic sense in every way. Tall and well made, with clean-cut limbs and features, fine smooth copper-colored skin, handsome face and features, heavy black hair done up in pompadour fashion . . . wide turquoise bead bracelets upon his upper arm, and a knife at his waist—this was my Charley."

Early the next morning, Ellen and Nellie were settled in an ambulance pulled by four mules for the trip to Fort Whipple. Saying goodbye to Martha and Jack Summerhayes, Ellen felt they "should have a medal for their services there, protecting the supplies that came into the Territory for the officers and soldiers, entirely surrounded by hostile Indians, and not much more than a corporal's guard to depend on aside from some Indian scouts."

Ellen found the country she rode through,

dry, sandy and sterile; the glare of light was so great that the sand-plains glowed beneath the glowing sun, and we travelled slowly. At mid-day we stopped for luncheon by what seemed to me the bottom of a creek, but the men dug down and found a little spring. The heat was intense. One could scarcely breathe. The very crows sat drooping and open-mouthed, too hot to caw, but when disturbed sailed through the brazen sky without seeming effort.

At two o'clock we were off again. There was no change in the character of the country; we could see for miles in every direction, the mountains looming in the distance. Toward night-fall it became a little cooler, and we camped near a small stream.

We had a complete camping outfit, which included a tent and some bed-springs on which to lay my mattress and pillow. Everything was as comfortable as possible, considering we were crossing a desert; Nellie and Mary [the nursemaid] were with me in the tent, while the Colonel slept on the ground near the men and close to my tent door, and although I knew I was in a country where the Indians were warlike I never had a calmer sleep than my first night on this great desert. I had great confidence in the soldiers of the Sixth Cavalry (who were there for my protection) who had fought so many hard fights against these Apaches, and no fear had yet entered my heart; alas, it was to come later.

In the morning we were up early; it was most beautiful, and as far as the eye could reach not a sign of life could be seen; we seemed to be the only living people on the planet. . . .

[W]e had a fine mess chest, and a dutch oven in which the bread and biscuit were baked. We also had an arrangement made of wire to put meat or game on to broil; the Colonel shot plenty for all of us, including escort, teamsters and ourselves. The out-door life was delightful; the desert seemed a wonderful place to me; already I was beginning to feel its atmosphere and no longer wondered at the gypsies. Nelly was as happy as a bird, and as well as possible.

Soon after breakfast we broke camp, and at eight o'clock were off for the day's march. The road was lined with cactus of every description, wonderful and beautiful to me, as the plains of neither Nevada or Colorado have this beautiful plant. There were also mesquite trees, a species of acacia which grow to the height of ten or twelve feet; the seeds, which are contained in a small pod, are used by the Indians to make bread; it is quite sweet, palatable and very nutritious. The wood of these trees is very hard and heavy. They were almost the only trees we

saw excepting the willows which grow by the little streams and
springs and where you generally find a ranch. . . .

As we had a mountain to cross which was very steep, the
Colonel, Nelly and Mary got out of the ambulance and walked
quite a distance and the escort dismounted and led their horses,
which were slowly walked. On reaching the summit the scene was
entrancing. The mountains stretched away on each side, and
some isolated peaks stood out in bold relief. We could see a stream
winding its way through a cañon; we stopped for a few minutes
only, as we had still a long distance to ride before reaching water,
but the silent picture will ever remain in my mind, as will the
wonderful sunset we saw that evening.

After a night under the stars, the company started early the next day
crossing "the desert until we came to a mountain that rose abruptly
from the plain and was crested with a wall some two hundred feet high
and was nearly perpendicular, forming one of the noted landmarks of
the country."

High mesas (mountains that have flat tops) closed in here and
formed a cañon through which we rode. The trail was narrow,
barely six feet wide. The mountain towered above us on our
right, and a deep precipice was on our left. It was very weird
and made me feel strangely as we crawled along, for the ascent
was difficult.

There was not a sound, only the tread of the mules and the
horses which the soldiers rode; not even a sound of insect life could
be heard. The stillness was of death; the tension terrible. It was
called "Dead Man's Cañon," not only because of the massacres
that had occurred there, but also because of the entire absence
of life, insect as well as animal. At about four o'clock we drove

rapidly down the cañon and turned into a beautiful valley. Here were hundreds of cacti in bloom—red, purple, yellow, and white. I uttered a psalm of thanksgiving, the sight was so beautiful, and coming as it did so unexpectedly upon me thrilled me, and it was with difficulty that I controlled my feelings. . . .

The country through which we travelled the morning of the third day was rolling, and there was a fine stream by which we stopped for an early luncheon. The Colonel as usual had killed plenty of game as it abounded near the streams. That afternoon we had a long march across the desert to get water for the night's camp, so we did not rest long, but started off and rode quickly to cross the long stretch of desert before night-time should overtake us.

Just before sundown two of the escort, one leading the Colonel's horse, rode rapidly back to the ambulance to speak to the Colonel, who was riding with me. He immediately got down to talk with them, and I knew it was about something serious. Whenever the Colonel rode with me, he had his rifle ready for instant use, as all of the escort had, but before riding off with the men, he took a pistol from its case and while hurriedly loading it, said: "The men see signs of Indians; I must ride ahead for a while." He handed me the pistol saying: "Keep courage and remember what I have always told you—never let an Indian take you alive."

A great lump rose in my throat; my head swam, and I was terribly scared, but almost instantly I thought of my child who must be protected; and the poor girl [Mary] who had braved danger in coming to make my journey across the desert more comfortable was in a panic of fear, so in trying to reassure her my own courage was somewhat restored. We rode very slowly on, each one filled with his own thoughts; ten minutes seemed an hour, and the sun was fast sinking in the western sky. Each moment I thought I could bear the suspense no longer.

We stopped, and it seemed an eternity before the Colonel returned, but I saw from his face, before he spoke, that he was somewhat relieved. He said: "There are signs of Indians, but I think they have passed on, and we will go on as rapidly as possible." Which we did, the escort remaining very close. That night we camped at a stage station, which we reached about nine o'clock. The Colonel asked if I would rather go in, and sleep in the house, but I preferred the tent, with the soldiers all around; but there was not much sleep for me.

The next morning we broke camp early; it was much cooler, and the country more settled. We passed several ranches and had a pleasant but uneventful day, the only thing of particular interest being the passing of the stage coach with the four horses on a run, carrying the mail; it was the only team of any kind we had seen since leaving Ehrenberg.

That night was our last camping station. We had a fine supper of biscuit, coffee, game, and potatoes. The moon came out bright (and it seems to be brighter and to give a softer light in that wonderful climate than anywhere else) and we sat long by the camp-fire, talking and singing.

Next morning we were off bright and early. We hoped to reach Prescott by two o'clock, and although I had enjoyed the outdoor life, and the wonderful country I had gone over, I was glad to reach our destination; but my little girl and the Colonel would gladly have kept on, notwithstanding it was thirty days since we had left San Francisco. He loved the out-door life and the shooting, and the little one was all unconscious of fear. . . .

We had to drive through Prescott, the capital of the Territory, to reach Fort Whipple. It was a small but well-built town.

There was a plaza, or park, in the center of the town and stores
on the four sides of it. One side was given up to the saloons; but it
was fairly orderly, considering it was a mining town. . . . I never
saw a place grow so rapidly and improve in every way as it did
during the five and a half years we lived near it. . . .

Such a welcome as we had! I had hardly gotten the dust from
my face and hands when General [August] and Mrs. [Fannie]
Kautz were announced, and soon after all of the staff officers and
their wives and many others from the garrison. Champagne was
opened and our health and hearty welcome drunk. The whole
afternoon was spent in going over old Indian fights and cam-
paigns, for here were officers who had served through the Modoc,
Sioux, Arapaho, Apache, and other Indian wars. Stories were
told of thrilling escapes and I, not yet recovered from the fright of
a few nights before, told of our alarm.

Initially, the Biddles settled in a small house until the officer and his
family living in the one assigned to them moved out. But Ellen was not
at all pleased with the living quarters at Fort Whipple. As she explained,
officers' quarters were

low, broad houses with hall in the center, and two rooms about
sixteen feet square on each side; pantry and kitchen back, also an
attic above. I often looked through the cracks in my house to the
light outside. They were built of wood and ceiled (as there was
no plaster to be had), and in that dry climate the wood shrunk,
leaving great slits for the light and air to come in and as there
was often in winter a difference of fifty degrees in temperature
between the day and night-time, we had to keep great fires going
continually. We had no stoves or furnaces; only the large open
hearth fire, and it is needless to say it was hard at times to keep

warm. We bought thin muslin, something like cheese-cloth, and had it tacked over the walls of the living-room, and bed-room and papered them, the muslin holding the paper, a soft gray ground with the passion vine and red flower in full bloom. We had sent to San Francisco for it, and it took just four months to reach us after the order was sent.

Although she found her living accommodations less than adequate, Ellen thoroughly enjoyed the variety of social events at Fort Whipple, quite different from her previous postings, noting it was "a very gay post, with an entertainment of some kind almost every day and evening. In fact years after we used to allude to the time when General Kautz was in command as 'the days of the Empire.'"

The General's wife, Fannie, was a musician, painter, and actress. She formed the Fort Whipple Theater in 1877, putting on shows such as "Dead Shot," and "Regular Fix," along with several Shakespearean dramas. When they performed "The Two Orphans," proceeds went to the Sisters of Charity, who built and ran Prescott's first civilian hospital. Some criticized the frivolousness of theater productions in the middle of Indian territory, but the officers and their wives thrived on societal activities that infused the fort.

Twice during her time at Fort Whipple, Ellen remembered attending a hop (dance) or play "when we heard the 'Assembly Call.' Every officer dropped his partner and ran to his troop, and in an hour's time they were in the saddle and off to catch the Apaches, who were on the war-path, killing and destroying everything they passed."

Ellen does not mention socializing with Lily Fremont, daughter of Arizona's fifth Territorial Governor John C. Fremont, who was living in the territory's capital of Prescott at the time, but Lily's diary comments on several visits with Ellen and her daughter during the year 1879.

"The days for the women were all alike," Ellen noted,

Usually in the morning we rode or drove, and we sewed a part of every day and ofttimes in the evenings, for as I have said we had all our own and our children's clothes to make, besides the adornment of our houses.

I remember very well upholstering a lounge and two chairs in pretty light blue cretonne with apple blossoms on it. . . . I also made window-curtains of the same material with fluted swiss ruffles, and lined with a soft unbleached cotton. They were very pretty and when they were drawn at night to keep out the cold, our room was charmingly pretty and cozy. Years after an officer told me there was not (to his mind) as pretty a room in Washington as my dainty little living-room on the frontier. This showed how little of the beautiful we had around us. In fact we would have been starved had it not been for the blue skies, the wonderful rugged mountains, and the mystery of the desert.

Misfortune struck the post on June 17, 1877, when Fannie Kautz delivered a stillborn girl she named Lillie. Four days later, Ellen delivered a boy, James Harwood Biddle. But the child died July 11, less than a month after his birth. The women buried their children in the Whipple Cemetery.

Although not always in the best of health, Ellen was seldom idle. Along with keeping her household running smoothly, she was instrumental in raising funds for the Sisters of Charity's hospital in Prescott and donated milk from her cows for the patients (she also raised hens, chickens, and turkeys). James, who sometimes enjoyed a game of poker when not on duty, promised to divide any of his winnings with the Sisters, which he did for a while until Mother Monica asked Ellen one day, "What has become of the Colonel? We have not seen him for a long time." "Ah! Well, then, Mother," Ellen replied, "he can't have been winning."

Nicholas Biddle was born at Fort Whipple on December 4, 1878. Mary, the maid who had ridden across the territory with the Biddles, had married an enlisted man, forcing the Colonel to hire a nurse for the baby and bring her out from San Francisco, paying the grand sum of one hundred dollars a month for her services. She stayed three months before moving on. Ellen requested her services again when she was expecting her seventh child. When asked if she would demand the same high salary, "The old lady dropped her head and thought for awhile," Ellen wrote, "then said, 'Well, madam, if you are going to make a yearly job of this, I guess I can come for ninety dollars per month.'" Insulted, Ellen chose not to hire her for the birth of Alice Wallace Biddle, who arrived in February 1880.

Relieved of his duty shortly after Alice's birth, James readied his family for his next post, Fort Grant, in southeastern Arizona.

"We left Fort Whipple one beautiful morning," Ellen noted, "December fourth [1880], Nick's birthday; he was just two years old. . . . I left with one long tender regret, for the grave of my little son [James] under the shadow of the great mountain had to remain."

The Colonel had fixed the middle seat nicely for Alice by lacing ropes back and forth quite high, so it was impossible for her to fall off. I had put soft pillows on the seat, and there the little lady sat during the journey as happy as a bird. Nick often got out and walked up the hills with his father and, although I had no nurse, I got along finely. The children slept soundly and gave me no trouble whatever. We went over much the same ground for nearly two days that we had passed going into the Territory, but it was much more settled and at peace; no sign of Indians off their reservations; and we never dreamed there could be such trouble as old Geronimo caused later.

The third day we reached Phoenix, a nice, clean town, all green and white, with trees planted on all the streets. They had

brought water in and ran all around in "acequias" (small ditches)
watering them. I am told that Phoenix is now a thriving city. . . .
Tucson is also in this southern part of the Territory. It is an
exceedingly interesting old Spanish and American city, irregu-
larly laid out and built in the usual style of adobe architecture.
It is pleasantly situated in the Santa Cruz valley, but it was not
very healthy at the time we passed by. [A smallpox epidemic per-
meated southern Arizona, including the town of Tucson, during
the late 1870s and early 1880s.]

There was also a fine military post, "Fort Lowell," and
a delightful society, Spanish and American. It was in this
southern part of the Territory that we saw the most remarkable
mirages, great cities and castles, and churches with domes; it was
almost impossible to believe they were not real.

Our journey was altogether delightful; no Indians, the
weather perfect, the children and myself well, and plenty of game
for the Colonel to shoot. We enjoyed every moment, and I was
sorry when we began our last day's march.

We arrived at Fort Grant about three o'clock in the after-
noon, and went at once to our own quarters, where we used our
camping outfit until the waggons [sic] arrived with the furni-
ture, etc. . . .

We had a nice double house, with courtyard in the center, in
the Spanish style. It was built of adobe, with three rooms on each
side opening out on a wide porch and garden; at the back of the
garden were the stables. The soldiers came and helped me get the
house in order. We took our breakfast at home, but went to the sut-
ler's for luncheon and dinner. I had no nurse, but we had an excel-
lent man who remained at the house while we went to dinner. . . .

Fort Grant was beautifully situated at the foot of Mount
Graham. The climate was perfect. I would spread a large com-

fortable [blanket] on the floor of the porch for Alice to play on, and we would be out-of-doors all the day long. I would sew or read and watch the children. At six o'clock the little ones had their supper by the bright hearth fire and would go to bed. A fire during the day was unnecessary, even in winter. . . .

The life at Grant was very simple and very healthful. I never have breathed such invigorating air. The winter days were full of sunshine, and the atmosphere was so clear that I could stand on the porch and see the trains come in and go out at Willcox, twenty-three miles distant.

Earlier in his career, James had been stationed at Fort Dodge, Kansas, where he may have acquired the friendship of a young, up-and-coming lawman, Wyatt Earp, who served as a policeman in Wichita and later assistant marshal of Dodge City. When the Biddles arrived at Fort Grant, James once again ran into Wyatt, who was leading a posse from Henry Hooker's Sierra Bonita Ranch located north of Willcox. At the time, Wyatt was a wanted man and James was tasked with preventing him from fleeing. But James was also loyal to his friends.

According to historian Casey Tefertiller in *Wyatt Earp: The Life Behind the Legend*, James told the lawman/outlaw, "Wyatt, I'm going to have to hold you here. They're looking for you and there are warrants out for your arrest. We're going to hold you. But come in and have something to eat first."

James ordered fresh mounts be tethered at a particular gate before he sat down to eat with the Earp gang. Later James excused himself and walked out of the room. Wyatt and his men finished their dinner before riding out of town on the horses James had conveniently left behind.

By this time, Ellen had sent eleven-year-old Nellie back east to school and she was determined to reunite with all of her children since she had not seen her two oldest sons for several years. As soon as the weather warmed up, she bundled up baby Alice and little Nick and boarded the train out of Willcox headed east.

"The journey from Fort Grant was filled with anxiety," she wrote. "My little daughter [Alice] was seriously ill from the change in the milk, and for hours after reaching New Mexico she lay in a state of collapse, from the high altitude. The dear Sisters of Charity were invaluable to me. We telegraphed ahead to have physicians meet us at the stations, which they did, and gradually the child got better."

Finally arriving in Philadelphia, she reunited with sons Jack and David. "They had grown almost out of my recollection," she exclaimed, "they were great tall boys, the picture of health. I gazed at them in astonishment and could scarcely believe they were the little fellows I had left six years before, and that they really belonged to me."

She and the children spent a blissful summer in the Blue Ridge Mountains, with its lush mountain range and temperate climate, but Ellen did not find it as appealing "as the great rugged peaks I had lived among so long."

"One day late in August," Ellen wrote, "I saw she [Alice] was not well and I sent hurriedly for a physician, who soon after his arrival sent for another, and I then knew my child's life was in danger. . . . [I]n two hours from the time the doctor arrived the dear little heart that had given so much pleasure to every one who had ever come in contact with her had ceased to beat." Ellen provided no information about Alice's illness or the cause of her death.

She took her children to Elizabeth, New Jersey, where they remained until the winter of 1885. The two older boys were now on their own and Nellie was attending school in Washington, DC.

In 1886, James was ordered to Fort Myer, Virginia, and eventually relocated to the War Department in Washington, DC. When he was sent west again in 1890, Ellen chose to remain with her children until James reached Fort Robinson, Nebraska, where she eventually joined him.

James retired from the Army in 1896 and was promoted to Brigadier General, retired, in 1904. He died in West Virginia in 1910. Ellen wrote her memoirs in 1907 and received wide acclaim for her portrayal of military life on the western frontier. She died in 1922 at the age of eighty-one. Both James and Ellen are buried at Arlington National Cemetery.

The Biddles's daughter, Ellen McGowan "Nellie" Biddle Shipman, became one of the first female landscape architects and is known for her formal gardens and distinctive planting styles. In 1933, she was recognized as the "Dean of Women Landscape Architects."

CHAPTER 7

A Calmness of Desperation

Katharine Sadler Madison Cochran

K atharine Cochran's journal, *Posie; or, From Reveille to Retreat: An Army Story*, published in 1896, presents a challenge as she wrote of her husband and children by using pseudonyms throughout the manuscript. Yet her description of events that took place at Fort Apache from 1879 through 1881 provides a riveting depiction of the dangers experienced by many military families.

In her memoir, Katharine called herself Posie, her husband was Captain Prescott, and the children assumed a variety of aliases.

"Two of the most uneventful, and at the same time eventful, years of my life, were spent at Fort Apache, Arizona," Katharine wrote. "Uneventful, because we were four or five hundred miles from everybody and everything, got our mail by buckboard once a week, then relapsed into our usual monotonous life, read and re-read our letters, exchanged papers, magazines, etc., with our friends, and discussed the topics of the day (two or three weeks old)."

Major Melville Augustus Cochran and his family lived in relative comfort at Fort Apache. "Our house was the only two-story building in the fort (the rest of the officers' quarters were one-story log houses, with low roofs). The day of our arrival at the post, as we passed a set of these quarters that had been partly built, Florida [daughter Anna] remarked, 'Oh, mamma, that must be the pigs' house.'"

Born in 1852, Katharine Sadler Madison married Melville Cochran in 1872 in St. John's, Florida. Fifteen years older than his twenty-year-old bride, Melville was previously married to Laura Etta Pray, who had died in 1866, leaving no children. Katharine and Melville had five

*Katharine Sadler
Madison Cochran*
Photo courtesy Julie
Kettleman, great-great-
great granddaughter of
Katharine Cochran.

children during their travels with the military; four were with them at
Fort Apache. Percy Madison Cochran (called Howard in Katharine's
journal) was born in St. Augustine, Florida, in 1873. Anna Cochran
(known as Florida in the journal) followed in 1875 while the family was
stationed in Mount Vernon, Alabama. Melville Cochran, Jr. arrived in
1878 during a stint at Fort Walla Walla, Washington, followed by William Cochran in July 1881 after they arrived at Fort Apache. William
survived less than two years. Katharine Cochran, or Kate as she was
called (Daisy in the journal), arrived in 1884 at Fort Keogh, Montana.

If this passel of children were not enough to keep Katharine occupied at Fort Apache, along with recuperating from the birth of William

the month after she arrived, she also had to protect her household during one of the most bloody uprisings that occurred between the soldiers at Fort Apache and White Mountain Apaches. Her account of the August 1881 incident differs little from official reports, but seen through a woman's eyes, the battle presented more danger to the fort, and its occupants, than mentioned in official versions.

"From the cold, bracing climate of Oregon," Katharine wrote as the family traipsed across barren wastelands to Fort Apache, "we found ourselves . . . on the arid deserts of Arizona, breathing and almost stifling in the dust that was thrown into the ambulance by the wind that always seemed to blow in the wrong direction. The water was strong alkali, and the children all got sick. We stopped at Yuma for a rest. Hearing that there were two hotels in the town, the Major asked a man which was better. 'Oh! It does not make any difference,' he replied, 'whichever one you go to, you will wish that you had gone to the other.'"

When we arrived at Fort Apache, with its good water and fine climate, we made up our minds to make the best of it, give up all idea of the outside world, and be as happy as it was possible to be under such circumstances. We had good horses, several cows, plenty of chickens, fine gardens and quantities of game, so, as far as comforts were concerned, we were well off. . . .

The valleys for miles around were filled with Indians camping and planting corn. It had been their custom, from time immemorial, to spend the summer months in the mountains and return to the lower country in winter. There was always more or less dread of them, and we never felt particularly safe when away from the post, although we often visited their various camps and watched their dances, etc. In August their "Green Corn" dance occurred, the ceremonies being very interesting. This year, of which I write [1881], they were unusually exciting. There appeared in their midst a Medicine Man (Nockadelcline), who claimed that he could raise the dead—a shrewd rascal, with a power as absolute as if he really was what he claimed to be.

The season was an unusually fruitful one. In every direction could be seen their fields, almost bending with the weight of the grain. Of course, with the prospect of such large crops, they were not careful of their old supply of corn and made large quantities of Tizwin, their native drink, which looks much like dirty buttermilk, and after starving themselves for two or three days, they drank large quantities and became very hilarious.

Things were assuming a very serious aspect around us. We could hear the sound of their tom-toms day and night, and although few of them now came into the post, we were well informed of their meetings.

Nockadelcline exacted large rewards from them for his services, such as money, blankets and ponies. At last he announced that their dead warriors were alive up to their waists, and that the only way he could complete the resurrection was for all the white people to leave the country. Of course, this to their already frenzied minds meant the war path. The commanding officer of the fort [Colonel Eugene Asa Carr], appreciating the dangerous condition of affairs, sent for Nockadelcline and some of the leading warriors to come in and have a talk, thinking that he could quiet them; but instead of coming, they moved their field of operations to the Cibecue, about fifty miles distant.

Then every one was more excited than ever, and rumors of war and danger came in from every direction. Finally, our gallant colonel decided to go after Nockadelcline and bring him back, a prisoner, to the fort, and in this way, if possible, save the lives and homes of the many settlers throughout the country.

The command consisted of two troops of cavalry, one company of infantry, and one company of Apache Indian scouts, the latter commanded by one of the young officers. The colonel started off with the cavalry and scouts, leaving the infantry company to guard the fort. There was not one in the command that left, nor one in the little command that remained behind, who did not have grave apprehensions for the future.

Only a few hours after the command left, Indians began following. They would pass through the fort, mounted and "armed to the teeth," twenty at a time, until it became so appalling that the officer who was now in command decided to send a courier to warn the colonel, one to warn the settlers living in the vicinity of the fort, one to bring in two soldiers who were in charge of the Black River ferry, twenty miles away, and one to go through to the nearest telegraph station with a dispatch, asking the commanding general for re-enforcements. . . .

About eleven o'clock of the second night, a Mexican, who had an Indian wife, and who had always lived with the Indians, came into the fort and reported that all of the "Nantans" (officers) and most of the soldiers had been killed, and that those left needed aid from the fort. The officers at once decided that the Mexican was a spy, and that it was only a trap laid to get the infantry into ambush and massacre them, so they again sent for the fellow to question him, but he had disappeared, although at first he said that he had come in for protection.

Every precaution had been taken to defend the fort, and an isolated set of quarters had been prepared with food, water, arms, and ammunition for our final retreat, where we hoped, with our fifty soldiers, a few citizens (and the women and children), to hold out until rescue could come to us.

Our greatest fear and anxiety now was for the cavalry command, for they had the roughest kind of country to go through and hundreds of well armed Indians to contend with. In the morning of the third day the telegraph operator volunteered to

go up to a high point of a mountain near by, where he could
command a view of the narrow pass to the north, through which
the troops had gone, and signal down if he could see any thing
of the command. Pickets were thrown out along his course to
defend him if possible. At last, after an hour or more of waiting
he signaled that "he could see two horseman [sic] advancing, but
did not know if they were friends or foes." Then, after another
interval of waiting, that "the command was in sight."

My dear reader, can you realize how we all felt! Can you
imagine what were the hopes and fears of those wives who had
been waiting two days and nights without sleep! The moments
seemed like hours now, for the command was still quite a dis-
tance off. Finally, the two horsemen that the operator first saw
rode up to the commanding officer's quarters, where many were
waiting in feverish anxiety and listened with throbbing hearts to
the report of the sergeant to the commanding officer.

Cibecue Creek lay about forty-five miles from the Fort Apache Indian
Reservation. Major Cochran was put in charge of the fort when Colonel Carr set out to arrest Nockadelcline. Carr found the medicine
man sequestered at the creek. After arresting Nockadelcline, and as the
soldiers made their way back to the fort, they were attacked by hostile
Apaches. Nockadelcline was killed along with his family and countless
Apaches. Seven soldiers perished in the onslaught.

"In a few hours we could see the Indians beginning to appear in
the vicinity again," Katharine continued. "A strong picket line was now
thrown around the entire post, and we felt comparatively safe, with our
numbers so much increased."

As night approached, we knew we had nothing to fear again
until morning, as the Apaches are miserable cowards, afraid of

darkness and ghosts. Nothing would tempt them out at night.
Early next morning, we could see hundreds of them down in the
valley, at the gardens, killing cattle, and having a war-dance.
Then the garden houses were fired, and altogether it was any
thing but a cheerful spectacle. We were now in a perfect state of
siege, entirely cut off from the rest of the world—the telegraph
wires down, the rivers swollen. We did not know whether five
hundred or five thousand Indians surrounded us, or whether
the couriers had succeeded in getting through with the dispatches
asking for aid.

About ten o'clock, an armed body of men was sent to the
grave-yard, a short distance from the fort, to dig graves. They
had no sooner arrived there than they were met with a perfect
fusillade from the hills near by. They at once retreated, firing as
fast as they could reload, and all got back safely. This was evi-
dently a signal for the attack on the fort, which was now begun
in earnest.

Across the cañon, in the valley, were some old adobe ruins,
which afforded them good shelter. From this point they kept up
a continual firing. The bullets would whiz past, but we were
well protected.

At this time, our youngest child [William] was four weeks
old. There were large adobe chimneys in the house. The children,
during the fight, were all made to sit or lie near one of the fire-
places, as they afforded a perfect breastwork against the bullets. . . .

From one of the upstairs windows of our house, I com-
manded a view of the entire fight, watched my husband under
fire for an hour or more, listened to the whiz of the enemies'
bullets and to the deafening storm from our own men. I could
see the Indians trying to make a nearer point, where they would
have better breastworks, see our men blaze away and the Indians

turn and seek cover, but not so in all cases, for I saw one of them throw up his arms and drop from his horse, as if dead.

There was a sentinel at our door day and night. I told him never to let the children, nor myself, be taken by Indians. He well knew my meaning, and I felt confident as I looked into his brave, determined countenance, that he would do his duty nobly if the time should come.

There was a calmness of desperation that seemed to settle over me, a calmness that can only come on such occasions. It is then that the soul knows itself, and communes with its God, feeling that at any moment it may be summoned into his presence.

There was little or no sleep for any one. Every few hours there was a new skirmish. An Indian had only to come in range for the whole picket line to blaze away. The men were excited and made over the loss of their comrades, so any Indian they got a chance at shared a hard fate.

The fourth night every thing seemed quiet, and those not on guard were trying to snatch what sleep they could, when, bang, bang, went a perfect fusillade, and the shrill notes of the bugle, which were almost drowned by the firing. Then almost in an instant the whole fort seemed ablaze. I surely thought that the end had now come, and as the men rushed out to extinguish the burning set of quarters, expected to see them shot down as they ran, but the enemy had withdrawn for the night, and no further loss was encountered save the one wooden building, which was burned to the ground.

The fifth day was comparatively quiet; only an occasional alarm. The Indians, seeing that they could do us but little harm, saved their ammunition and amused themselves cavorting around out of bullet range, and gorging themselves on the settlers' cattle.

About eleven that night we could hear a disturbance and noise on the top of the mountain, back of the soldiers' quarters, from which point a narrow trail led into the fort. Every one thought that the Indians had awakened from their fear and superstition, and that we were in for a night attack. There seemed great indecision from those above as to what they should do, although there were, evidently, large numbers. Every man below was on the alert, waiting and watching. They only wanted a signal to blaze away.

Finally, some one suggested re-inforcements [sic] and the bugle sounded its loudest call. Then, from above, almost as a voice from heaven, came the welcome return notes and we knew that friends were coming. The pass was so narrow, steep and rough, that it was almost impossible for the horses to be brought down, but they had come by trail as it was the shortest way to reach us.

From the brow of the mountain, they could see the smoldering ruins of the garden-houses. Large amounts of grain had been stored there, by contractors, which kept the fire bright for many days. The Indian guides insisted that it was the site of the fort, and that every one had been killed and every thing burned. The soldiers had almost to push them along to make them go further, as they said all of these soldiers would be killed too, and they wanted to turn back. This was the cause of the confusion that we heard, as they insisted that they would not descend into the valley. Our joy was great at seeing them march in, but, if possible, theirs was greater at finding us alive.

They said nothing could describe their feelings when looking on the smoldering ruins, and believing that it was all that was left of those they had known and loved. They had determined to push forward into even the jaws of death until they found out the fate of those whom they had come to rescue, for even if the command had been massacred, some of the women and children might be alive and prisoners.

Of all the couriers sent out only one got through. The road was lined with dead bodies for miles; every one had been killed who happened on it those few fatal days. The two soldiers at the ferry were also lying dead. The weather being very hot the stench from the unburied bodies was something dreadful. In a very few days large bodies of troops began to come in from other parts of the territory, and from New Mexico, and we had nothing more to fear.

Two weeks after the Cibecue battle, Major Cochran was ordered to report to Fort Whipple in central Arizona. Katharine, relieved to be leaving this place of murder and mayhem, gazed in awe at the surrounding countryside as she traveled along the Mogollon Rim, a two-hundred-mile stretch that embodies terrains from northern pines to the desert floor. "The country was as silent as the sentinel," Katharine wrote.

There was something appalling in the grandeur of the scenery. As far as the eye could reach there seemed to be a sea of mighty mountains, while the vicinity showed evidence of volcanic fires, with vast beds of lava forming innumerable shapes, fantastic and real. One could walk through what seemed to be an immense field of small rooms, with walls as perfect as if only waiting to have the roof adjusted. Here was the place of all places for the children, and they immediately went to "housekeeping," playing "Swiss Family Robinson," and insisting on staying indefinitely there, for never would there be such play houses again.

As they settled in for their first night on the road, thoughts of what they had just endured at Fort Apache invaded Katharine's observations.

A tent was pitched with the flap opening in front of one fire-place, thus giving the children and myself a private, comfortable room. Supper was cooked on the other fire. The men who were not on guard rolled up in their blankets on the dirt floor and soon forgot their cares. Our little ones were as sweetly sleeping as if in their own beds at home, but there was no rest for me. I was exhausted; the weird place oppressed me, and the sad, uncertain rustling of each "wooly curtain" thrilled me, filled me with fantastic terrors never felt before; but to still the beating of my heart, I kept repeating, "tis the wind and nothing more."

[The next day], the "going" was so rough that the wheels of the ambulance did not seem to touch the ground for miles, but jumped from rock to rock. The children were laughing and joking, seeming rather to enjoy the bumping and shaking up they were getting, when, quick as a flash, Florida [Anna] leaned out of the window just as the ambulance gave a terrible lurch, and out she went under the wheels. It was all so quickly done that we scarcely realized what was the matter.

The Major called to the driver, "Stop the mules! Stop the mules!" Our Chinese servant, who was in front with the driver, seized his gun, exclaiming "Heap Injin! Heap Injin!" as we jumped out. We could see lying in a heap among the rocks, our darling. The Major soon had her in his strong arms, and we poured water on her head and called her name again and again. Then the dark eyes opened and her lips began to move. "Oh, Papa, I did not mean to lean out so far!" . . . A large rock had evidently turned the wheel out of its course, and, by the position she lay in, we could see that her escape was a miracle. She was only stunned, and after a short time was bright and strong again.

As the wagons made their way into the Verde Valley, the troops "camped in the vicinity of Montezuma Well, one of the most noted [sights] in the territory. It lies at the base of a perpendicular cliff, with the opening of the dwelling just over it. The occupants could come down on a ladder, procure water, and on their return drag up the ladder after them, thus making their peculiar home secure against intruders."

Deriving its name from a natural spring that exists on the land, Montezuma Well is a water hole that dates back thousands of years. Scientists believe an ancient cavern collapsed and formed a limestone sinkhole that contains high concentrations of carbon dioxide and alkali, preventing fish from living in the spring.

Sitting 100 feet below the desert floor, the well spans about 470 feet across and descends to a depth of around 50 feet. Millions of gallons of water a day flow through the basin, with the water retaining a constant temperature of 76 degrees.

Prehistoric Hohokam and Sinagua Indians are believed to have used the spring to irrigate crops of corn, beans, and squash. Western Apaches relied on the ancient waters to nourish their gardens until they were driven out by encroaching white settlements.

Soldiers who first saw the spring wrongly assumed the Aztec ruler Montezuma had ridden this far north, maybe even settled in the area. Montezuma, however, never ventured into central Arizona, leaving the lake misnamed to this day.

"We did not tarry long here," Katharine noted, "for we were nearing civilization. Before many days the faint notes of a bugle came floating to our ears, and we were soon within sight of our new home. That first glimpse of the quarters, the parade ground and the flag, made Whipple Barracks seem most attractive after days of 'roughing it.'"

We were soon settled in our cosy [sic] quarters. Whipple Barracks was an ideal western post—a large command of infantry with headquarters and band, besides department headquarters and a busy little town only two miles away [the beginnings of the town of Prescott], or, perhaps, not quite so far, with many nice people who made it agreeable for the army people. There was a continual round of gayety, luncheons, dinners and hops, which were an agreeable change from our long quiet. The officers would meet often at our house, smoke and discuss various subjects. The older ones often turned to the war and their many experiences. Howard [son Percy] was always wild to be where he could hear them.

After two years at Fort Whipple, Major Cochran was ordered to Fort Keogh, Montana, where their last child, Katharine Cochran, was born in 1884.

The major retired from the military in June 1898. The family lived for a while at Fort McPherson, Georgia, before retiring to Florida. Katharine died on August 26, 1903, and Melville followed her on May 4, 1904. Both are buried at Arlington National Cemetery, home to heroic soldiers and their stalwart spouses.

PART IV

Enlisted Men's Wives, Servants, and Laundresses

Corporal Casey was not at all pleased when his wife was evicted from Fort McDowell for disobeying an officer's order to wash the family clothing. Mrs. Casey had been hired as a laundress by the Army and she had her hands full taking care of the dirty laundry of about fifteen soldiers as well as the commanding officer. When another officer ordered her to add to her burden by washing his family's attire, she refused to comply. The officer banished her from the fort.

Reluctantly, Mrs. Casey moved into the town of Phoenix, about twenty miles away. Phoenix in 1884 boasted a population of about 2,500 inhabitants, not the booming metropolis it would someday become.

Angry at losing his wife, and knowing that as a hired laundress for the military she was entitled to housing, food, and the services of the post doctor, amenities she could not take advantage of while living off post, Corporal Casey appealed to his commanding officer. The matter eventually ended up on the desk of General George Crook, head of the Department of Arizona. Discussions and allegations resulted in Mrs. Casey being accused of immoral character and Mrs. Casey claiming she was too ill to take on the extra burden. Mrs. Casey won her case and the corporal gratefully fetched his wife and brought her back to Fort McDowell, where she resumed her duties as a laundress for the Army, without adding the other officer's dirty clothes to her already heavy load.

The only women with any official status on a military post were laundresses hired by the Army, usually the wives of enlisted men who chose to travel with their husbands wherever they were sent, and to supplement their husband's meager salaries by working as washerwomen.

The Laundress circa 1800s Library of Congress, LC-USZ62-77778

The Army, however, discouraged men from marrying at all and provided scant accommodations for those who did bring their wives and
children with them. In fact, in 1869, Brevet Brigadier General Henry D.
Wallen, who named Arizona's Fort Wallen after himself, published a booklet detailing when and how enlisted men could marry. *Service Manual for
the Instruction of Newly Appointed Commissioned Officers, and the Rank
and File of the Army, as Compiled from Army Regulations, the Articles of
War, and the Customs of the Service*, was not a popular document among
the men or their potential wives as evidenced by the following regulations:

> *Neither non-commissioned officers nor soldiers are to marry
> without the consent of the commanding officer.*
> *Any man marrying without permission, both from his com-
> pany commander and from the officer commanding the post or*

regiment, will not be entitled to receive any of those indulgences bestowed on such as marry by consent.

It is impossible to point out in too strong terms the inconveniences and evils which follow a regiment encumbered with women and children. The washing in a company will provide for a certain number of women—about one for every twelve men—but beyond that, distress and poverty must ensue.

Officers should, therefore, do all in their power to deter their men from marrying beyond the rule laid down; and, however hard they may at the moment consider such denial, there are few who will not, after a short period, feel thankful to them for it.

Every woman connected with a command should be required to make herself useful to it in some way, either in washing, sewing, or knitting. This applies particularly to the laundresses of companies who receive rations and quarters, and who should be examples of industry, propriety, and good conduct. Any woman found on trial to be useless, should not be allowed to remain on the strength of the command.

Women, whether they were the wives of enlisted men or single women who followed the military from one post to another serving as laundresses, received payment for their services from the government. They were provided a place to live (although the housing allotted was usually substandard), rations, and the amenities of the post doctor. As a laundress, an enlisted man's wife was allowed to accompany her husband at the expense of the military when he was relocated, and the income she earned washing clothes certainly contributed to the betterment of the family. It was, as Mrs. Casey contended, not an easy job.

Serving from 1802 until 1878, laundresses were part of the Army long before they were on the payroll and continued to work for some time after Congress eliminated the position. As the military moved into western territories, the number of washerwomen increased, with more laundresses documented than at any other time. An 1841 regulation allowed four laundresses for each company with each woman receiving "one ration per day." They were paid out of the men's wages by a company clerk to ensure they would not be cheated by a soldier who liked clean clothes but preferred to spend his meager salary on something other than his wash.

Military posts offered poor accommodations for the wives of enlisted men who served as laundresses, with housing usually situated on the outskirts of the main compound. Dubbed "Suds Row" or "Sudsville," this collection of lodgings frequently ran the gamut of an assortment of low huts, tattered tents discarded as unlivable, crude dugouts, and even caves—anything that afforded a semblance of shelter.

The quarters for enlisted men and their families at Fort McDowell in 1874 consisted of adobe huts covered with brush that were situated near the periphery of the post. Fort Yuma offered the same lowly accommodations.

The military offered laundresses one meal a day and, depending on where they were stationed, this repast might consist of a pound of salt pork or bacon, some beef, flour, cornmeal, beans or peas, hominy or rice, coffee, tea, sugar, salt, pepper, and vinegar. The meat was too tough to fry or roast, which meant it had to be boiled to make it edible, sometimes a blessing since refrigeration was almost nonexistent on remote desert posts and the meat often spoiled before being doled out. Fresh vegetables and fruits could occasionally be purchased from the sutler's store but were often too expensive for enlisted families to afford. Scurvy from lack of citrus was prevalent on many outlying garrisons.

Laundresses usually washed a soldier's clothing three times a week in the summer and twice a week during winter months. On many southern Arizona posts where temperatures were consistently hot and often humid, laundresses kept to the three-times-a-week schedule year-round.

Women brought with them or purchased their own supplies although the Army provided a few necessities such as wooden tubs and the fat to make soap. A sutler's store might carry some form of soap but it was expensive, particularly in the West, forcing many women to make their own suds. They would save the fat from their own meals as well as procure fat from the post's butchered animals for soap making.

Each wash and rinse could require up to fifty gallons of water. The women hauled their own water from the nearest source, which could be quite a distance in western territories since streams were not always nearby. And even if there was a close water supply, it might not run year-round depending on the local rainfall. They also chopped their own firewood unless they could persuade a soldier to help out.

Laundresses were hired to wash the clothes of enlisted men but they could take on the additional task of an officer's laundry, or even better, an entire officer's family, at a high enough wage to offset the extra work involved. Mrs. Casey felt her workload heavy enough and she was not inclined, or obligated, to add to her chores.

As the wife of the post doctor at Camp Date Creek, Fanny Corbusier brought along her own cook and maid. When her maid quit, Fanny was faced with washing her own clothes. She was ill equipped for the task. "I washed, dried, and starched them as I thought was right," she said, "but they were so stiff that I could not get them off the lines . . . I could not help crying as I carried water from the barrel in the kitchen to loosen them. . . . I couldn't do that work again." Fanny's husband went to the post commander who ordered one of the Army laundresses to add the Corbusier washing to her already heavy load. Unlike Mrs. Casey, the laundress agreed, probably because it meant more money in her family's coffers.

The wives of enlisted men had little chance of advancing their social status, even if their husbands rose through the ranks to become officers. The men might enjoy the amiability of other officers, but their wives would never be considered equals by officers' spouses. Labeled "half-way ladies" because of their inability to break through societal ranks their husbands enjoyed, most of these women lacked the refinement and education to be considered on a par with officers' wives. Officers' wives were more than willing to offer kindly advice to these women but rarely did they strike up any sort of friendship.

With their husbands earning about thirteen dollars a month, and if they could not get hired on as a laundress, an enlisted man's wife looked to find work in the home of an officer serving as a cook, maid, nurse, or nanny. Since most officers' wives insisted on having servants, these women became a ready source of hired help.

Single women, whether arriving in the territory on their own or brought in by a relative to help with children, be companions for a lonely wife, or to cook and clean, rarely lasted long before attracting the eye of an eligible bachelor soldier and marrying within months of arriving.

Single enlisted men were considered good servants also. Commonly called strikers, these men mainly worked as cooks, which added additional funds to their income. A striker could earn an extra five or ten dollars a month as a good cook. By 1870, however, the military stopped allowing officers to use enlisted men as servants, although for a while afterward, the regulation was ignored.

Martha Summerhayes adored her striker, Bowen, who not only put her kitchen in order but prepared appetizing meals. At Camp Apache, she was delighted when, "A cooking-stove and various things were sent over from the Q.M. [quartermaster] store-house, and Bowen (the wonder of it!) drove in nails, and hung up my Fort Russell tin-ware, and put up shelves and stood my pans in rows, and polished the stove, and went out and stole a table somewhere (Bowen was invaluable in that way), polished the zinc under the stove, and lo! and behold, my army kitchen.!'" One would think Martha readily put on her apron and got to work, but she admitted she was a terrible cook with her only culinary contributions the making of quince jelly and floating islands.

Families sometimes hired Native help, with mixed results. Ellen Biddle attempted to educate a teenage Apache boy in the intricacies of working as a servant. She dressed him in white man's clothing and taught him to wait on her guests around the table. She was delighted with his progress but eventually the boy ran away and returned to his people. When Ellen saw him again he had reverted to his Native dress and customs.

Evy Alexander took in an Apache girl and was pleased with how well the child adapted to her new life. When the girl took a shine to Evy's newborn daughter, Evy decided she would "keep her and raise her for a nurse for little Midge."

By 1876, the military was questioning the feasibility of keeping laundresses on the Army payroll. When officers were asked their opinions on the practicality of retaining the women, responses varied greatly. General William Tecumseh Sherman concluded that soldiers should wash their own clothes while others feared enlisted men would leave the military as soon as their tour of duty was up if their wives and children could not accompany them and provide a sobering family influence. Many commanders acknowledged that their best and most efficient men were those married to laundresses.

Adjutant General John Kelton understood the necessity of having women and children support their husbands, fathers, and brothers as they marched across unrelenting deserts and faced unknown dangers to serve and protect the growing populace on the western frontier. "It has been discovered ages ago," General Kelton argued, "that no community of men can prosper where there are no wives and children . . . the influence of these women and their helpless families is of incalculable advantage to the men of garrison, cut off for years from home influences . . . wives and children at military posts are just as ennobling and necessary to the soldier as to men in any other condition of life."

In the end, Congress abolished the position of laundress in 1878, although they allowed women to continue the practice until their husbands left the military. And since enlisted men's wives continued to follow their husbands long after they were no longer paid to wash clothes, the practice took several years to completely disappear. After that, civilians were used as laundresses until 1901, when the military authorized the operation of laundries on posts.

Most enlisted men's wives were poorly educated. Some could read and write but many were illiterate. Recorded histories left by these women are rare. Nevertheless, what is known about them warrants recognition and acknowledgment along with the other women who braved uncharted territory.

* * *

When US President James K. Polk ordered Zachary Taylor to defend Texas against an invading Mexican Army, he authorized the inclusion of fifty-five women to cook, clean, and wash for the troops. Sarah Borginnis, also known as Sarah Bowman along with a handful of other appellations, rode with General Taylor and his troops, and later served the Army at Fort Yuma. Much of her life is recorded as idealistic legend, yet we know she marched with the soldiers across Texas and Mexico as well as serving in Arizona. She was a giant of a woman who even took up arms herself when the fighting became intense.

Jane Thorpy, a complete contradiction to the larger-than-life Sarah Bowman, was a good-natured, affable Irishwoman who followed her husband across the country during the Civil War and out west. Throughout the fourteen years her husband was with the military, she bore six children while serving as a laundress on at least nine different posts. As with Sarah, Jane probably had little formal education, yet she cared for her family as only she knew how—with her rough, raw hands scrubbing the dirty clothes of the military under sometimes unimaginable circumstances.

CHAPTER 8

The Great Western

Sarah Bowman

Just one thin sheet of sandpaper separated Yuma from Hell, according to Sarah Bowman, a woman reputed to be of immense size who followed the Army across Texas and Mexico before settling along the Colorado River near Fort Yuma. Over six feet tall and weighing close to two hundred pounds, the buxom red-haired beauty earned a reputation as a hard-working, astute businesswoman even though she could neither read nor write, although she did speak fluent Spanish. Toiling as a laundress, cook, and nurse for the military, usually with a couple of pistols strapped around her waist, her status among the soldiers was one of awe and fear. One of them reported her as a "[r]emarkably large, well proportioned, strong woman of strong nerves and great physical power, capable of enduring great fatigue." Another supposedly christened her the Great Western after the world's largest steam-powered ship at the time.

Where she came from remains a mystery as assorted accounts list her born sometime between 1812 and 1817 in either Tennessee or Missouri. She acquired several husbands during her lifetime and went by a variety of surnames such as Bourdette, Bouget, Bourjette, Borginnis, Davis, and Phillips before uniting with Army Sargent Albert Bowman, whose name she kept the rest of her life.

Her first husband, according to Sarah, was a soldier stationed with Brigadier General Zachary Taylor's Army as Taylor marched into Florida to take part in the Seminole Indian Wars around 1837. Sarah signed on as a laundress and cook.

In 1846, as Taylor's troops made their way along the banks of the Rio Grande to stave off an approaching Mexican army threatening to reclaim

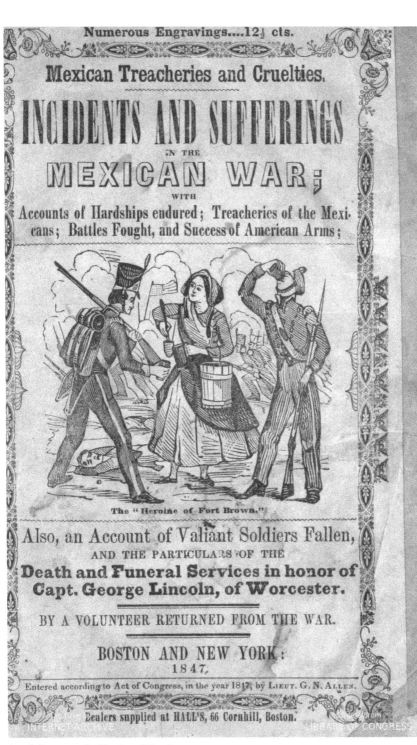

Numerous Engravings....12¼ cts.

Mexican Treacheries and Cruelties.

INCIDENTS AND SUFFERINGS

IN THE

MEXICAN WAR;

WITH

Accounts of Hardships endured; Treacheries of the Mexicans; Battles Fought, and Success of American Arms;

The "Heroine of Fort Brown."

Also, an Account of Valiant Soldiers Fallen,

AND THE PARTICULARS OF THE

Death and Funeral Services in honor of Capt. George Lincoln, of Worcester.

BY A VOLUNTEER RETURNED FROM THE WAR.

BOSTON AND NEW YORK:

1847.

Entered according to Act of Congress, in the year 1847, by LIEUT. G. N. ALLEN.

Dealers supplied at HALL'S, 66 Cornhill, Boston.

Sarah Bowman, the Heroine of Fort Brown Allen, G. N. [from old catalog]. *Mexican Treacheries and Cruelties: Incidents and Sufferings in the Mexican War; With Accounts of Hardships Endured.* Boston and New York, 1847.

Texas, Sarah was with him, hauling her wagonload of pots, pans, and laundry equipment across the rough terrain.

Arriving on the north bank of the Rio Grande, Taylor ordered the construction of a stronghold that was originally named Fort Texas and eventually became Fort Brown. Taylor went on to Point Isabel, leaving a small troop to defend the newly built post. Sarah remained at Fort Texas to cook and clean for the soldiers.

When General Mariano Arista realized the fledgling fort was poorly protected, he crossed the Rio Grande with his troops and laid siege on the handful of men left to defend the garrison.

For five days and nights the battle raged with Sarah smack in the middle of the action, defying orders that all women at the fort (about ten or twelve) seek shelter from the fusillade of bullets.

Sarah started her cooking fires and set up her kitchen near the center of the garrison, ready to serve strong, hot coffee and nourishing meals to those defending the fort. If the men could not leave their posts, she made her way to the stronghold walls with steaming cups of coffee to fortify the troops.

Allowed to charge for her services, Sarah took nothing for her meals while the fort was under fire. She even asked for a musket so she could replace wounded soldiers on the walls. "[T]he cannonballs, bullets and shot . . . were falling thick and fast around her," read one report. "She continued to administer to the wants of the wounded and dying; at last the siege became so hot that a bullet passed through her bonnet and another through her bread tray."

When the smoke cleared, and after Taylor arrived with fresh troops, Arista was defeated. As bravely as the men had fought, it was Sarah who received recognition and was touted as the Heroine of Fort Texas.

The Army moved across the Rio Grande into Matamoros, Mexico. Sarah went with them and that summer, she started a restaurant and boardinghouse in the little Mexican town. Soldiers appreciated and enjoyed Sarah's meals and the entertainment she provided wherever she set up one of her establishments, relishing much tastier food than the military provided.

When Taylor and his troops headed farther south toward Monterrey, Sarah and her wagonload of goods followed along. She survived a bloody four-day battle to take the town, working in the field as she had at Fort Texas, helping doctors with the wounded and cooking up a mess of beans for the men. Reportedly, she also made bullets for the troops.

She opened the American House in Monterrey, providing all the necessities a battle-scarred soldier could desire: food, liquor, and the company of obliging women. Yet that fall when Taylor headed west toward the town of Saltillo to take on General Santa Anna, she packed up and moved with him, establishing another American House where one soldier said he "paid $2.50 for my entertainment at the boarding house of the Great Western."

"She was a great nurse," claimed another soldier, ". . . would always get up at night at any time to get one something to eat."

The battle with Santa Anna was brutal and during one skirmish, some of Taylor's troops deserted. One of the fugitives made his way back to Sarah's hotel with the panicked message that Taylor was going down in defeat. Sarah, who absolutely adored Zachary Taylor, soundly punched the man in the face. "You damned son of a bitch," she shouted, "there ain't Mexicans enough in Mexico to whip old Taylor. You just spread that report and I'll beat you to death." Those who witnessed the confrontation quickly returned to the battlefield.

The US–Mexican War lasted two years, ending the summer of 1848. As the troops pulled out, Sarah prepared to go along, but since she had shed her husband somewhere along the way, she was told she would have to marry one of the soldiers before she could continue to serve as a laundress and cook. Undaunted, Sarah informed commander Major Daniel H. Rucker, "All right, Major, I'll marry the whole Squadron and you thrown in but what I go along."

Sarah then mounted her horse and rode down a line of soldiers shouting, "Who wants a wife with fifteen thousand dollars, and the biggest leg in Mexico! Come my beauties, don't all speak at once—who is the lucky man?" Most were too stunned to react, but one soldier named Davis accepted the offer if a clergyman could be found to make the union official. "Bring your blanket to my tent tonight," Sarah laughed, "and I will learn you to tie a knot that will satisfy you I reckon!" Sarah had found her next husband and continued to travel with the Army.

In the spring of 1849, Sarah was running another of her hotels north of the Rio Grande in a small community called Ponce's Ranch that would later become the town of El Paso.

She showed up in Socorro, New Mexico, in 1850 with a passel of children in tow. Somewhere along the way, she had acquired five young girls ranging in age from two to sixteen. Where these children, whose last name was Skinner, had lost their parents remains a mystery, but Sarah took them in and watched over them for many years. One of them, Nancy Skinner, called her Mother.

While in Socorro, and minus the husband she had acquired in Monterrey, Sarah met and may have married Sergeant Albert J. Bowman, who was stationed with the Second Dragoons (no record has been found of their union). When he was discharged from the Army in late 1852, the couple, along with the Skinner children, headed for the goldfields of California. They made it as far as Fort Yuma.

Having relocated to its present site in early 1852 under the leadership of Major Samuel Peter Heintzelman, Fort Yuma sat atop a hill on the California side of the Colorado River. Almost as soon as she arrived, Sarah signed on to cook and clean for the officers. Albert worked as a carpenter.

Major Heintzelman found this large, overbearing woman totally objectionable, but his men swarmed around her and offered good pay for her services. Heintzelman kept his distance, yet he jealously noted in his journal, "The Western as she calls herself, had a dinner yesterday and everybody in camp but me was invited. She sent to me for butter."

The officers as a group, minus their commander, hired Sarah to cook for them for twenty dollars a month, good pay along with her laundry duties.

Eventually Heintzelman succumbed to Sarah's charms and soon became one of her staunchest supporters, dining with her regularly. "I sent the Western a couple of nice watermelons for our dinner," he noted in his journal.

That spring, Heintzelman reported Sarah came to him claiming someone was trying to abduct two of the children she had living with her. She wanted to move across the Colorado River into Sonora, Mexico, to protect the youngsters. Heintzelman helped her relocate, although he wrote in his journal, "I can't see what she expects to do for a living when she moves over there."

Sarah's distance from the fort did not deter her from performing her duties as she continued to cook and clean for the military while establishing a boardinghouse and restaurant in Mexico, outside the Army's jurisdiction. Heintzelman noted, "The Western will send all her family over [into Mexico] and she with her washerwoman and cook will stay and keep the mess." Apparently, Sarah had help with the laundry and the meals.

Sarah knew exactly what she was doing by moving into Mexico. If she stayed at the Fort, she would have to abide by Army rules, and that hurt her business. She may have contrived this ruse in order to ply her trade as she wished. Still close enough to the fort for soldiers to enjoy their free time at her place across the border, Sarah offered as usual— good food, strong whiskey, and willing women.

Heintzelman soon realized Sarah had made him her fool. "The Western is making a convenience of us," he wrote. "She gives us what she pleases to eat and spends the whole day across the river." No one seemed to mind but the major.

In December 1853, the United States purchased almost thirty thousand square miles of land from Mexico. The Gadsden Treaty was ratified by Congress in June 1854. This acquisition put Sarah's boardinghouse back in the United States in what was then New Mexico Territory. Ten years later, this land became part of Arizona Territory. Accordingly, Sarah is presumed to be the first Anglo woman to live and run a business in the town of Yuma.

As Yuma began to grow, Sarah and Albert signed a contract to make seven hundred thousand adobe bricks for the construction of public buildings. Sarah marked the agreement with an "X" since throughout her dealings with the Army, she never learned to write.

She was still working at the officers' mess on February 22, 1856, when eighteen-year-old Olive Ann Oatman walked into Fort Yuma after surviving five years in Indian captivity. Olive and her sister, Mary Ann, had been captured after an Indian attack on the Oatman family as they made their way west across the desert to Fort Yuma. Mary Ann did not survive in captivity, but Olive was returned by the Mohave people who had bought her from her captors. Sarah cared for Olive until her brother, Lorenzo, who had survived the massacre of the Oatman family, came for her.

That October, Sarah and Albert left Fort Yuma for the bustling town of Tucson that then boasted a population of around one thousand hearty souls. By the following spring, however, Sarah, whose trade depended on the military, had moved closer to the newly established Fort Buchanan near Sonoita Creek.

Fort Buchanan was poorly constructed with most housing consisting of rough thatched huts or jacals affording little ventilation. Dirt floors and dirt ceilings provided scant protection from the weather and the variety of insects and reptiles that permeated the area. The post was abandoned in July 1861 and burned to the ground to prevent approaching Confederate troops from utilizing its amenities.

Sarah may have still been at Fort Buchanan in March 1860 when Tonto Apaches captured two women in the Santa Rita Mountains just south of the garrison. The post captain, Richard S. Ewell, sent troops to rescue ten-year-old Mercedes Saiz Quiroz from the raiding Apaches, but the Indians had left the other woman, Larcena Pennington Page, for dead in the mountains.

Subsisting on little but grass, seeds, and wild onions, Larcena, stripped of her shoes and warm outer clothing, survived by crawling down the mountain on her hands and knees, a feat that took her two weeks to accomplish.

By late 1860, Sarah was back working at Fort Yuma, and within the year, troops began the trek east to participate in the War Between the States.

Fort Yuma had little to do with the Civil War except to house troops passing through. One young recruit noted his first visit from Sarah when he arrived at the post on his way east:

At the time of arrival at the Fort, Feb, 1863, as I was sitting in front of my room trying to eliminate some of the dust acquired during my 300 miles tramp; I was accosted by a large American woman, a six footer, and proportionately broad with: "Lieutenant have you any washing you want done?" I hastened to hand her the only change of shirts I had. I enquired who she was and was informed she was the best known woman in the American Army. . . "The Great Western." . . . She was a splendid example of the American frontier woman.

After Arizona became a separate territory from New Mexico in February 1863, Territorial Governor John Noble Goodwin ordered a census of the populace. Albert Bowman's name appears on the census as a single man, occupation miner, living in Yuma. Sarah's name does not show up on the census but since she was then working and living at Fort Yuma, on the California side of the Colorado River, she was probably not counted in the Arizona census. When the couple separated is not known but since Albert was at least fifteen years younger than Sarah, he may have been looking for a fresher bride, as evidenced by the addition of Mary A. Bowman to his household by 1866.

Fort Yuma had its share of desertions and thefts as did many early posts. Conditions were harsh, pay and housing substandard. Thievery became so rampant at Yuma that by 1864 almost everyone was under scrutiny. Sarah was never suspected of stealing from the military, but she was certainly aware of many misdeeds. When asked to testify about what she knew, her statement proved damning against several officers. According to her testimony, officers ordered her to supply miners with military goods whenever they asked, adding, "It was almost an every day thing to see Mules, and 'burrows' packing Flour away from the Post."

During her time traveling with the military, Sarah worked as a cook, laundress, hotel and restaurant owner, madam, and heroine. She also claimed she had served as hospital matron at Fort Yuma for over ten years. She raised sheep to feed post personnel, corralling them in the fort's graveyard, declaring her sheep did a good job of keeping the grass shorn in what was already becoming a dilapidated, poorly managed cemetery.

Sarah was probably in her early fifties when she died on December 23, 1866. The cause of her death is undocumented except in soldiers' records that noted her passing. Most say she succumbed to a tarantula or spider bite. She was given full military honors, including a three-gun salute, and lauded by the first Bishop of Arizona, Jean Baptiste

Salpointe. She was buried in the Fort Yuma Cemetery beside the soldiers she had fed, nursed, and cared for as only she knew how, the only woman ever buried in the graveyard.

"Blunt and unguarded in speech," reported a California newspaper of her passing, "she was yet the possessor of a kind heart, and whatever her failings, engendered by wild associations, very many will remember with grateful feelings the acts of tenderness bestowed by her on themselves and associates in that inhospitable section. Always at the bedside of the sick, she cared for them as none but a woman can, and nothing that money or care could furnish was neglected by her."

In 1890, the old Yuma cemetery was in dire disrepair and the 159 bodies buried there were reinterred at the National Cemetery Presidio in San Francisco. Sarah went with the troops as she had throughout her life.

CHAPTER 9

Boiling Cauldrons

Jane Earl Thorpy

I rish-born Jane Earl Thorpy arrived in New York City in 1855. Where she came from in Ireland is unknown, but she had married her sweetheart in Dublin the previous year, July 24, 1854. Twenty-two-year-old John Thorpy set off almost immediately for America, leaving his bride to follow in about a year. The Thorpys never had much money, particularly since John spent much of his life as an infantryman in the US Army. He enlisted on January 8, 1855, shortly after arriving in the United States.

Born around 1836, Jane was not yet twenty years old when she married and followed her husband to America. She also went wherever John was ordered by the military. "I was always with him," she said, "and my occupation was doing laundry work for the officers and comrades of the company . . . ."

Jane signed on as a laundress with her husband's unit, allowing her to travel with him—most of the time.

While the popular adage that an army marches on its stomach is undoubtedly well founded, it was the laundresses who followed the early troops across the country who kept them clean and comfortable. Laundresses were usually the wives of enlisted men who needed the additional income to provide for their families. Jane, who bore six children at various posts around the West, certainly needed the extra money to supplement her husband's meager wages.

Enlisted men earned about ten to thirteen dollars a month, which was enough to get by if single, living in a barracks, and eating Army rations. But if man added a wife and children started arriving, he had to find additional sources of income.

Enlisted men were discouraged from marrying at all but that rarely stopped a determined husband and his blushing bride. Some soldiers kept their marriages secret while others sought permission from their commanders before tying the knot. Once married, the women were allowed to travel with their husbands if they could be of use doing chores such as washing, cooking, or acquiring a position in an officer's household as a servant.

While the military provided transportation, rations, and housing for the enlisted family, the housing was of poor quality and hardly fit for occupancy on some of the early posts. At both Camp McDowell and Fort Yuma, married enlisted men were often ensconced in crude adobe huts, unhealthy accommodations by any standards.

Initially stationed in New York, John Thorpy was soon ordered to Corpus Christi, Texas, where the couple's first child, daughter Mary Ann Thorpy, was born at Fort Belknap on September 25, 1857. The laundry area at Fort Belknap lay between the guard house and the stables, certainly no place for young children.

The following February, John was relocated to Camp Floyd, Utah, but Jane did not go with him. They were apart for two years, not reuniting until September 1859 at Camp Floyd after Jane made her way 1,100 miles along the Oregon Trail along with seventy-five other laundresses. She may have been stranded at either Jefferson Barracks in Missouri or Fort Leavenworth, Kansas, during this time.

Jane washed the clothing of single enlisted men as well as officers, their wives, and families, earning from each anywhere from $1 to $2.50 a month. If she was lucky enough to procure an entire family's laundry, she could make about $7 a month.

Jane also had to make her own soap using a combination of lye and meat fat. Lye was made from a mixture of water hauled from a nearby stream or river, and ash, preferably from a hardwood tree such as oak. As the liquid was drawn off, additional ash was added before pouring the liquid back over the ash. The more often this process was repeated, the stronger the lye. It took a trained eye to know how strong to make the lye. If too potent, the clothing would be ruined.

Each gallon of lye took about two pounds of grease, which usually consisted of beef or mutton tallow. The fat was cut into small pieces, heated until liquefied, then strained to remove any solids remaining on the fat. (Jane, like most laundresses, probably cooked these leftover pieces of meat into a meal for her family.) Lye was added to this concoction. When sufficiently boiled, the mixture was poured into molds and left to harden. Again, an experienced laundress knew when the soap was the correct consistency.

The entire process took hours to complete standing over hot boiling cauldrons. And it made no difference to the military if the laundress was pregnant or had several children to tend to—her job came first.

Jane gave birth to a son, John Thorpy, Jr., in "Alberkirk," New Mexico in 1861, but the child died sometime before 1870. William Thorpy arrived in 1863 while his father was stationed at Fort Union, New Mexico.

John mustered out of the army in 1864 and the Thorpys returned to New York City until John reenlisted in 1865, attaining the rank of sergeant. By November, they were on their way to southern Arizona's Fort Mason by way of the Isthmus of Panama, traveling steerage for $165 per adult and $96.75 for each child. The Army probably paid John and Jane's passage but the couple had to come up with the money for the children's fares on their own, a large sum for anyone at that time, but especially difficult for an enlisted man to raise. They went by way of Aspinwall aboard the ship *Baltic*, crossed the Isthmus by train, and boarded the ship *Sacramento* for California.

A month later, the family landed in San Francisco, sailed down the coast aboard the *Orizaba* for Los Angeles, and headed across the desert, arriving at Fort Mason on March 1, 1866, with three children in tow and Jane heavily pregnant with their fourth. Son James Joseph Thorpy arrived two months later.

Fort Mason, originally named Camp Moore in 1856, lay at the site of the Mexican Presidio de Calabasas, today part of the Tumacácori National Historic Park. It became Fort Mason in 1865 and was abandoned in the fall of 1866. While serving there, John and Jane were probably housed in a tent or one of the old abandoned buildings that were scattered across the nearby Gandara ranch, which had been abandoned in 1855. Along with two other women, Jane is listed as a laundress on the Fort Mason books.

With the abandonment of Fort Mason, John was sent to Camp Lowell. He was discharged from the service at Camp Wallen in 1868. Initially, Camp Wallen had been established to prevent the Apaches from traveling back and forth to Sonora, Mexico, but the Apaches soon found an alternate route for their forays and the post was abandoned in 1869.

John and Jane bought property in Tucson near Camp Lowell, probably the first house they ever owned. When Jane gave birth to another son in 1870, they named him John Thorpy, Jr., indicating the first John, Jr. had died. Unfortunately, this son also died within a year of his birth, maybe from the ravages of smallpox that was prevalent throughout southern Arizona at the time, particularly in Tucson.

Three of the Thorpy children, William, James, and the second John, Jr. were baptized at Tucson's San Augustín Church by Father Frances Xavier Jouvenceau, the first vicar general of the Catholic Diocese of Tucson.

With the death of one son, and the almost tragic loss of another who was reported to have fallen into an uncovered well in March 1871, the Thorpys decided to leave Tucson. They put their house on the market including all its contents and sold everything for one thousand dollars. By December, they were on their way back to New

York City. Their last child, daughter Jane Thorpy, was born in 1873 in New York but did not survive.

For his years of active duty in the military, John received a pension of eight dollars a month and after his death on May 19, 1899, Jane was provided a widow's benefit of the same amount. Moving in with her daughter Mary Ann and her husband, as did her son, William, Jane died in New York City on February 24, 1905. She had spent her life toiling for the health and betterment of her husband and children. Her raw, rough hands were all she had to show for her years of servitude.

PART V

ON OUR WAY HOME

Once Camp Date Creek closed in 1873 and Fanny Corbusier's husband received orders to relocate to the Verde Indian Reservation, considered an undesirable and unhealthy expanse at the time, Fanny decided it was time to take her children back to a more civilized environment. She arrived in Ehrenberg that September expecting to board a stagecoach that would take her to Los Angeles (Fanny does not elaborate on where she crossed the Colorado River.). Instead, she found her carriage consisted of a single-seat buckboard. And although she anticipated a decidedly lengthy but hopefully uneventful journey, Fanny soon discovered she had one more heart-thumping, wild ride to contend with before her Arizona days were behind her.

Placing two-year-old Claude next to her on the front seat of the buckboard and cradling nine-month-old baby Harold in her lap, Fanny settled in for a long day. Before the driver swung himself onto the wagon next to Claude, he wrapped a leather strap around Fanny and the children to keep them from falling out of the wagon, a forerunner of the modern-day seatbelt.

As the driver headed out, he grimaced and shook his hands. Fanny realized the man's hands were inflamed with cactus spines as he had fallen into a cholla cactus a few days before taking the reins of the buckboard. Finally, no longer able to hold onto the straps, he "took Harold on his lap and passed the reins to me," Fanny said, "wrapping the ends around the lower part of his wrists to be safe."

For forty miles to the next stage station, Fanny maneuvered the spirited horses while keeping a close eye on her two children under the driver's care. As they pulled into the station, the driver "complimented me on my driving and told everyone how much pluck I had. . . . The children, particularly Claude, thought it was fun."

"The driver and I talked of Arizona," Fanny said, "and what it might be in years to come, when there was water with which to irrigate the land, as he knew there would be."

Women left Arizona Territory with a sense of relief, a feeling of accomplishment they had survived their time in the Wild West, and sometimes with a pang of regret.

Elizabeth Burt recalled few pleasant memories of her time at Camp McDowell in 1886 and was more than relieved when her husband received his marching orders to relocate. She recalled vivid memories of the rattlesnake that crawled up between the floorboards of her house and led her on a merry chase before being corralled and subdued. She recounted "the numerous scorpions and centipedes that overran the old adobe walls of the kitchen; the monstrous tarantulas that were killed every now and then in the vicinity, and how our shoes each night were carefully filed [sic] with paper or other material to prevent an invasion from these repugnant and venomous creatures."

Evy Alexander, despite the disagreeable conditions she endured during her years at Fort McDowell, admitted the post was one of her favorites. There was, however, a purpose behind her liking the remote destination. In a letter to her mother she admitted that she preferred Arizona Territory to a more desirable location at the time because the far reaches of the wilderness gave her husband credit for hard duty, a burden that might lead to more peaceful and hopefully less isolated surroundings on their next tour.

Involved in missionary work most of her life, Evy wanted to relocate to the cool pines around Prescott as she was interested in establishing a church in the area. Before she left Fort McDowell in 1869, she doled out Bibles to the Indians and was "anxious to finish my work before I leave."

When military wives looked back on their time trudging their belongings, and their children, across blazing desert asphalt, up lofty elevations, and through unknown territories, some realized how fortunate they were to have experienced such amazing adventures. Most were quite young when they came west, full of dreams and expectations. The circumstances they faced changed them from demure eastern Victorian women into independent, courageous human beings who feared very little after their years living under sometimes primitive conditions.

In most of their journals and letters home, women dwelt not on the more difficult times they experienced, or the children they lost along the way, but instead focused on the novel environment in which they found themselves, the unique vegetation discovered only in the West, and the vigor of their surviving children who readily adapted when they were uprooted and relocated. And almost every one of these women felt they had contributed to the betterment of a post by their presence, a sentiment not always shared by those in command. Yet they persevered in following their spouses across uncharted lands and made the best of whatever circumstances they encountered. For some, leaving the territory proved more difficult than they ever imagined.

Alice Grierson spent only four months at Fort Grant and was reluctant to leave in the fall of 1886 when orders came for her husband to take command of the District of New Mexico in Santa Fe. She dreaded selling her furnishings that included a carriage, horses, and a flock of chickens. "I don't suppose I will like it there as well as I do here," she wrote to her son that November. "This elevation suits me better than a higher one, and besides being a new and good house, this is a very pleasant one . . . these are *the best* we have had in the army."

When Martha Summerhayes returned to the territory in 1886 after being gone for ten years, she found she did not like some of the changes she observed. Traveling by train to Tucson on her way to Fort Lowell, a luxurious mode of transportation compared to the days she bounced about in an Army ambulance, Martha barely recognized the town. "Everything seemed changed," she said. "Iced cantaloupe was served by a spick-span alert waiter; then, quail on toast. 'Ice in Arizona?' It was like a dream, and I remarked to Jack, 'This isn't the same Arizona we knew in '74, . . . I don't believe I like it as well either; all this luxury doesn't seem to belong to the place.'"

It took Martha a while to admit she missed her years in Arizona, but as she penned her experiences long after she left the territory, remembering the days she spent on some of the most remote outposts, she realized how much she yearned once again to visit and explore the arid wasteland. "I did not dream of the power of the desert," she wrote, "nor that I should ever long to see it again. But as I write, the longing possesses me, and the pictures then indelibly printed upon my mind, long forgotten amidst the scenes and events of half a lifetime, unfold themselves like a panorama before my vision and call me to come back, to look upon them once more."

* * *

Mary Adams spent three years in Arizona before her second lieutenant husband, John Quincy Adams, was ordered from Fort Bowie to Oregon. As she headed by buckboard across the territory one last time toward

Officers' quarters at Fort Bowie circa 1885 Arizona Historical Society, Places-Ft. Bowie Photo File, #25607

Fort Yuma, she had no idea she would soon be in fear for her life as well as that of her infant daughter. Their wagon train raced against almost insurmountable odds to outdistance raiding Apaches they encountered on their final trek across the western frontier.

Alice Sargent spent several years at Fort Huachuca, plus a short stint at Fort Apache. Her adventures with the Army took her "from the golden shores of the Pacific to the bleak New England coast, from the Green Mountains of Vermont to the palmetto groves of Florida, and from Cuba to the far away Islands of the Philippines." She was an amazing woman with a zest for life and adventure. Her travels around the world demonstrate the flexibility of military wives to adjust and adapt to whatever circumstances they encountered.

CHAPTER 10

---•••---

The Indians Are Surrounding Us!

Mary Wildman Adams

Mary Adams left an indelible record of a narrow escape she endured as she departed the territory in 1871. In 1894, she wrote about her ordeal for *The Midland Monthly*, titling the incident "An Arizona Adventure."

Mary was born in 1844 in Clarksfield, Ohio. In December 1867, at age twenty-three, she married Second Lieutenant John Quincy Adams, who had distinguished himself during the Civil War and was now on his way to Fort Bowie in Arizona Territory with the First US Cavalry. Mary followed him, arriving in late 1868.

Established in 1862 to ward off Apaches who terrified pioneers traveling through Apache Pass in Southeastern Arizona, Fort Bowie was rebuilt in 1868 on a more level ten-acre plot of land. The threat of Indian attacks persisted over the ensuing years as the Apache warrior Cochise raided nearby settlements, outlying farms, and ranches. The First Cavalry, commanded by Captain Reuben F. Bernard, was sent to Bowie to reinforce the garrison.

Troops engaged the Apaches on numerous occasions over the next few years and Lieutenant Adams saw his share of bloodshed and deprivation. Captain Bernard was an old hand at chasing Apaches, having served as commander of Camp Lowell before relocating to Fort Bowie. Bernard would eventually attain the rank of Brigadier General for his meritorious actions against the Apaches at Chiricahua Pass in October 1869, an event in which John Adams participated.

Mary and John remained at the fort until 1871 when the First Cavalry received orders to report to Oregon. By then, Mary had given birth to their first child, Marietta Adams, who was born at Bowie in August 1869.

The company headed out of Fort Bowie, with their destination over 350 miles away, along the banks of the Colorado River and Fort Yuma. They would travel over a desert that offered little shade, scant water, and unknown dangers. Leaving Fort Yuma, they had to cross the Colorado River and go on to San Diego before starting north to Oregon. Captain Bernard, along with his wife Alice and four-year-old son Harry, accompanied Mary, John, and little Marietta.

Alice Bernard probably dreaded the trip back through Fort Yuma. Her daughter Fannie Eugenia Bernard had been born there in December 1868 but only survived a few months, dying in Tucson the following March.

Mary's account of the journey mentions the party left Fort Bowie in February 1870, but she was off by one year as the troops actually departed in February 1871.

"Six mounted and armed soldiers, our escort, were close behind the ambulance," Mary wrote as the wagon train headed out. "At a little distance four army wagons, containing baggage and two or three discharged soldiers, with the driver, brought up the rear."

Our minds were filled with pleasant anticipations as we waved a merry good-bye to friends gathered to bid us God-speed.

After the first long, weary day's ride and we were gathered around the camp-fire, our joy had not diminished, for Arizona was a good place to emigrate from in those days. Happy talk and laughter passed the time, till we were admonished by the lateness of the hour that we must separate for the night. We went to our cozy tents for sleep and rest preparatory for the morrow's long ride. We did not dream how hard and full of peril it would be!

The early morning found us with refreshed minds and bodies and we again started in the same order of march, with song and jest. The morning hours were fast passing, when we were suddenly startled into silence by the sound of shouts and of firearms in the direction of the wagons. We could see nothing, for they were hidden from view by a slight bend in the road. We breathed again when some one said, "It is only the men firing at coyotes."

But the relief was only momentary. A soldier came running to us exclaiming, "The Indians are surrounding us!"

While speaking, he was endeavoring to extract an Indian arrow which had pierced his shoulder.

The officers held a hurried consultation.

Mrs. B [Alice Bernard] and I bound the poor fellow's bleeding wound as well as possible with the meager materials at hand, and making a pillow of shawls and wraps we laid him upon the bottom of the ambulance. Before this was accomplished other men came and reported the rest of their comrades killed.

But our danger was not yet over. Several miles further on, at the foot of the Pecacho mountain [probably Picacho Peak, about twenty-five miles north of Tucson, considered one of the most dangerous sites for Indian raids], was a narrow pass. Our hearts stood still when we realized the possibility that the Indians, mounting the mules they had taken from the wagons and riding through a short-cut, might intercept us at this pass.

We hastily prepared to start. Lieutenant R [Gerald Russell of the Third US Cavalry, who had been stationed at Fort Bowie also] and my husband still took the lead, but now the soldiers were distributed about the ambulance, two at each side and two at the back, each soldier with one of the men from the wagons on the horse behind him, and in the ambulance the fainting, dying soldier at our feet. Thus we began our mad race for life.

How the ambulance swayed and rocked, as the driver urged the horses into a gallop! And how bloodless was every man's face as he leaned forward in his saddle, with revolver ready in hand, peering behind each rock and bush for a hidden foe! The brave, steady eyes assured us that every one of them would die to defend the women and children.

Only God heard the agonizing prayers uttered as we sped along that dreary Arizona road—prayers for deliverance from a horrible death, or if captured, from a more horrible life.

As we neared the pass, every eye was strained to catch sight of the dreaded forms; but we passed on and into the open plains unmolested, and our peril was over.

That night our little company, gathered around the fire in the stage station, was very quiet. I thought sorrowfully of the three brave men whose bodies lay out in the moonlight, alone and uncared-for; but my heart also overflowed with a joy too solemn for words; for, though we had lost every worldly possession except the clothing we wore, what cared I for such loss! Was not my husband sitting there beside me? And was not a dear little sunny-haired baby sleeping peacefully upon my bosom?

Overjoyed to be leaving Arizona, Mary looked forward to a more peaceful post in Oregon, where she gave birth to another daughter, Charlotte Adams, whose date of birth is recorded as February 1871. If the year is correct, Mary was heavily pregnant as she made her way across the Arizona desert. It would not be uncommon for her to omit any mention of her condition.

On April 11, 1873, John, serving as chief signal officer, accompanied General Edward Richard Sprigg Canby and other negotiators to meet with the warring Modoc, who wanted to return to their homeland. The Modoc, upon learning from Canby they could not reach a peaceful settlement, pulled out concealed weapons and killed Canby and the other peace commissioners. John, watching from outside the negotiating tent, had the onerous task of reporting Canby's murder.

In 1875, Mary gave birth to a son, but young Harry Adams only lived a few years, dying at age six while the family was stationed in Fort Vancouver, Washington. His grave marker states he was the only son of John and Mary Adams.

Over the years, Mary traveled by her husband's side whenever possible. He was part of the Nez Perce uprising that lasted from June through October 1877, and by 1890, he had made his way to the winter campaign against the Sioux in South Dakota.

Retiring from the Army in 1896 with the rank of captain, John accepted an appointment with the War Department as Professor of Military Science and Tactics at the Culver Military Academy in Culver, Indiana. Mary must have been delighted that her days of wandering over dry, dusty, dangerous lands were finally over.

Mary and John spent their final days where they first met in Norwalk, Ohio.

Mary died on April 12, 1917 at the age of seventy-three. John died two years later. Both are buried in the Woodlawn Cemetery in Norwalk.

CHAPTER 11

---•●•---

We Were Young and Life Was Sweet

Alice Carey Applegate Sargent

On May 22, 1843, Anthony Lindsay Applegate, along with his wife, Elizabeth, and their six children, joined one thousand men and women traveling from Missouri to Oregon along the Oregon Trail. This was not the first wagon train to make the two-thousand-mile trip, but it was the largest group of pioneers to date to set out on a journey that would last several months. Not all of them survived.

More than one hundred wagons, plus five thousand oxen and cattle, accompanied these hardy souls who set out seeking new lands and new beginnings.

Alice Carey Applegate would not arrive until the family settled in Oregon, but the wanderlust of her parents stayed with her as she journeyed with her military husband for more than thirty years, experiencing the sights, smells, and conditions of Army posts across the United States, in Cuba, and in China. She loved practically every minute of her adventures.

The tenth of twelve children, Alice was born in Douglas County, Oregon, in 1852. The family soon moved south along the Siskiyou Road, where Alice's father operated the tollhouse over the Siskiyou Trail that traversed from southern Oregon into northern California.

"Looking back to that time," Alice wrote in 1921, "I realize that it was a wonderful experience for a child. Every day the road was thronged, there were immense freight wagons drawn by six and eight yoke of oxen, towering Marietta wagons drawn by six span of horses. . . . Twice daily the great red and yellow stage coaches went swinging by. . . . There were long trains of travel stained immigrants with their weary ox teams. . . . I must not forget the wagons loaded with apples on their way to the mining towns in California. The wagon boxes were lined with straw and the apples piled into them. These apple peddlers advertised their fruit in a unique way by having a pointed stick fastened to a corner of the wagon bed on which was stuck an apple."

On August 11, 1886, Alice married Second Lieutenant Herbert Howland Sargent, newly graduated from West Point. She was six years older than her husband, but this made no difference to Alice as she adored the handsome Herbert.

The couple had no children of their own but they either adopted or fostered one son, Warren Lynch, although the child is not mentioned in Alice's memoirs.

"During my thirty-two years with the Army," Alice wrote in her 1909 journal, *Following the Flag: Diary of a Soldier's Wife*, "I followed the flag from the golden shores of the Pacific to the bleak New England coast, from the Green Mountains of Vermont to the palmetto groves of Florida,

Alice Carey Applegate Sargent
Photo Courtesy Southern Oregon
Historical Society, #7580

and from Cuba to the far away Islands of the Philippines—a life brim full of thrilling and interesting experiences . . ." She explained that her diary only touched "on the high lights in these eventful years."

Several of those years were spent in Arizona Territory, mainly at Fort Huachuca in southern Arizona. Herbert was later sent north to the Apache Indian Reservation, and on to Fort Bowie.

Herbert was stationed at Fort Klamath, Oregon, at the time he and Alice married, but shortly after their nuptials, he received orders to teach military science and tactics at the University of Illinois at Urbana–Champaign. A year later, he was ordered to Fort Bidwell, California.

In October 1888, the couple was again on the march from California to Fort Walla Walla, Washington, a five-hundred-mile trek that began at the onset of winter.

"I decided to go with him," Alice wrote, "as I had a splendid horse of my own, a horse I had bought at Bidwell and of whom I was very fond and very proud. This horse was called Patsy; he was a beautiful dark mahogany bay with a white star in his forehead."

The first week or so of our march was delightful, weather ideal and good camping places. Cavalry on a march have a certain rule as to gait; walk, trot and gallop, walk, trot and gallop. This change of gait rests both men and horses. In the afternoons the trumpeter would blow "Dismount" and the troopers would walk and lead their horses. Usually this order to dismount would be given at the top of some long, steep grade. I used to slip out of my saddle and lead my horse, and when the order came to mount I got into my saddle, feeling quite rested and ready to ride the remaining miles to camp.

The pleasantness of the journey soon waned as the weather turned from brisk fall to a chilling winter storm. "I could not keep my hands and feet warm while on horseback," Alice lamented, "and reluctantly found refuge in a covered coach called a 'Dougherty' wagon, my horse being led by one of the troopers. . . .

"The weather finally became so cold our sandwiches would be frozen and not fit to eat. We fell back on hardtack; two or three pieces of hardtack would keep us up until we went into camp and could get a good, hot supper."

The couple stayed eighteen months at Fort Walla Walla before receiving orders to report to Fort Huachuca, Arizona Territory, in 1890, a significant contrast to the cold winter months of Washington.

According to Alice, "We did not much relish the prospect of going to Arizona, for many and lurid were the tales that were told of the dreadful heat, the sand storms, the Gila monsters, centipedes, tarantulas, etc., but when Uncle Sam said 'March,' we marched."

Situated about fifteen miles north of Mexico, Fort Huachuca was established to secure the border as well as deter Chiricahua Apaches from threatening the area. By the time the Sargents arrived, however, the Indian Wars were almost over.

Of all the posts Alice and Herbert experienced, Alice proclaimed Fort Huachuca their favorite. "We met the sandstorms, to be sure," she wrote,

we also found the Gila monsters, centipedes, tarantulas, and many other creeping and crawling things, but the extreme dryness of the atmosphere tempered the heat, we were six thousand feet above sea level, the winters were mild and delightful, the ranchers were glad to let us have cows to milk for their keep. True, the renegade Apache, called "The Kid," terrorized the ranchers and outlying settlements and detachments had to be sent out frequently to chase the "Kid" and his band of outlaws. Sometimes my husband, with a small command, would be out for a couple of weeks; nevertheless, we were young and life was sweet.

Considered the most feared outlaw in Arizona during late 1880s and early 1890s, the White Mountain Apache Kid had, at one time, been a trusted scout for the Army. He was now a convict on the run.

The Kid and his band were accused of gunning down ranchers, and stealing cattle and horses. In March 1890, shortly before the Sargents arrived, a freight hauler was murdered near Fort Thomas. In August, three men were killed at Hachita, about fifty miles southwest of Lordsburg, New Mexico, all supposedly at the hands of the renegade Kid. He was never caught.

While stationed at Fort Huachuca, Herbert spent several months on temporary duty on the Fort Apache Indian Reservation in northeastern Arizona. Alice went with him and was captivated with the process set up to monitor the White Mountain Apaches:

The heat was very great and sand storms were frequent, but we found it [Fort Apache] rather interesting. Friday was issue day and by daylight the Indians fairly swarmed in to get the supplies given them by the Government. Beef cattle were slaughtered on the spot and each head of a household received his or her share. The Indians were formed into long lines, moving in single file; each Indian in line carried a card, giving the number of persons dependent on this particular individual for support. As the tickets were presented at the door of the commissary storehouse so many pounds of flour, sugar, tea, rice and beef were handed out, the amount of each according to the number of dependents on the ticket.

When my husband was off duty we used to go over to the Indian camps looking for baskets. Some of these were very artistic and beautiful. The Colonel carried his revolver and I carried a club. This weapon was used to protect us from the Indian dogs which were quite numerous and sometimes ferocious.

Returning to Fort Huachuca after their stint at Fort Apache, Alice and Herbert enjoyed their time on this southern Arizona post until orders came to report to Fort Bowie, which had been established to ward off hostile Indians threatening travelers going through Apache Pass near the New Mexico border, and to protect the only water supply for miles.

In 1898, Herbert received orders to report to Washington, DC, to help organize volunteers off to fight in the Spanish–American War. Alice had no intention of remaining behind when her husband sailed for Santiago, Cuba. Her description of the time she spent in Cuba, and the Philippines is in sharp contrast to the years she lived in Arizona Territory.

"On August eighth at three o'clock P. M. we sailed from Savannah, Georgia," she wrote, "on board the transport Rio Grande, Captain Staple, for Santiago de Cuba. On the vessel were six hundred and fifty-five men and officers of the 5th U. S. V. Infantry, part of Colonel Sargent's regiment of Immunes, so called. The voyage across was a very pleasant one, a smooth sea and very few cases of sea sickness."

The hillside military camp afforded pleasant city views, but the rains kept Alice inside her tent home far longer than she wished. "For some days food and water were scarce," she noted, "and we were delighted to get a tin cup of coffee and a bit of bread for our breakfast."

Despite the weather, Alice found Santiago attractive and scenic, yet not without its distractions, somewhat similar to those she experienced in Arizona.

This island is beautiful, mountainous and green to the very summits. Villas nestle among the trees and the white tents of Uncle Sam's boys cluster on the hilltops. But the sun is intensely hot and the air seems full of hot steam. A scorpion on my skirts, and a small snake in our Lieutenant Colonel's tent warned us to keep our eyes open for creeping things. The mosquito toots his small horn, while tiny flies drive our poor horses almost wild.

She was delighted when she found General Adna Chaffee among those on the island. Alice had met Chaffee during her time in Arizona and had dubbed him the "Iron Duke." Chaffee rose to fame during the Civil War before fighting on the western frontier.

That fall, those pesky mosquitoes spread yellow fever throughout the camp, with Alice and Herbert helpless victims of the scourge. By the following summer, she claimed she was the only woman in camp. When Herbert was ordered to take command of the District of Guantanamo, sixty miles away, she hoped for better living conditions than in Santiago.

"Here I had a house to live in," she wrote jubilantly. "After eight months of tent life it was a pleasure. This house had been the home of a Spanish officer at the beginning of the war, and in it we found five coal-black cats which my Barbadoes [sic] maid declared were the ghosts of Spaniards left to guard the place."

Returning to the States, Alice was not yet through with international travel. In October 1899, Herbert sailed for the Philippines, but the Army refused to allow women on military transports. Alice had no intention of being left behind.

She finally found passage to Manilla by way of Hong Kong, a decidedly long route, but that did not deter a determined woman. In December she sailed out of San Francisco for Hong Kong, spent the Christmas holidays at sea, and arrived in Manilla by late January 1900.

While in Manila, Alice enjoyed a bit of notoriety by writing a series of articles about the country for an Illinois newspaper, the *Carlinville Democrat.*

In 1901, Alice and Herbert left China, but shortly after landing on American soil, they were on their way back to Cuba. When they returned to the States this time, Herbert was ordered to Fort Ethan Allen, Vermont, and from there he taught at the Agricultural and Mechanical College of Texas for four years. He went to Fort Des Moines, Iowa, then to South Dakota, before heading to Washington, DC, and San Francisco.

Alice and Herbert made one more trip to the Philippines before Herbert retired. They returned to Oregon and settled in Medford but both "missed the trumpet calls and the boom of the sunset gun."

Moving to Jacksonville, Oregon, they thought their lives were fulfilled, but the Army had other plans.

In 1916, Herbert was recalled to active duty to serve during World War I. Again, Alice deemed to go with him. She had journeyed almost around the world beside her husband and witnessed her share of grief and disaster although she did not dwell on these aspects of her travel. A world war could not dissuade her.

"Of course I was not required to go with him," Alice said, "but it was the logical thing for me to do. I had always gone with him, and I could not reconcile myself to being left behind."

She took training classes in first aid expecting to join the Nursing Cadet Corps, but at age sixty-three she was informed she was too old to enlist. Herbert would not have her at his side on this tour of duty.

After the war, Alice and Herbert returned to their home in Oregon where they lived until Herbert's death in 1921.

Herbert's military career spanned the globe and he is remembered as an intellectual tactician. He taught military strategy in colleges across the country and wrote four books while on duty around the world. To honor her husband, Alice had a rock wall erected in his memory along Cemetery Road in Jacksonville.

In her later years, Alice wrote articles about her travels as well as historic accounts of her native state. She was active in the Native Daughters of Oregon and a founder of the Jacksonville Museum, forerunner of the Southern Oregon Historical Society.

Alice died on March 1, 1934, at her home in Jacksonville at the age of eighty-two. For her service during the years she spent traveling thousands of miles around the world to dozens of military posts, she was bestowed a full military funeral.

EPILOGUE: TAPS

———•••———

T he military wives who came west with their husbands into relatively uncharted territories in the mid- to late 1800s were not the
same when they returned east. No longer were they docile and delicate;
they feared little after what they had witnessed and endured on their
journeys across vast wastelands. Their husbands were often surprised
at the differences in their wives. From the young women they had taken
west, they had to acknowledge their spouses were stronger in body,
mind, and spirit, and could handle almost any incident or event that
crossed their trails. They were resolute in their fortitude to build better
homes for their families, determined that their children become well-ed-
ucated, respected citizens regardless of the circumstances under which
they sometimes lived on remote, isolated Army posts.

Military wives offered a moderate, often gentle touch on military
forts upon which they settled. They sewed curtains to soften mud-
brown walls; covered rough, wooden tables with elegant tablecloths;
and polished silverware to brighten up a dim, sometimes windowless
room. They grew fruits and vegetables and nurtured flowers to bloom
in barren soils. They brought new life to the frontier through the children who came with them as well as those who arrived while living on
barren outposts. They established a feminine, refined society within the
confines of masculine-governed garrisons.

They struggled through deep sands and walked up lofty elevations,
only to see the same treacherous passage before them for miles yet to
conquer. It was this persistent struggle to forge ahead that gave them

great respect for the very environment that altered their lives. While dreading unknown dangers that awaited over the next hill or just beyond the confines of a fort, most found something to admire and enjoy as they overcame unfamiliar and unpredictable surroundings.

In *Campfollowing: A History of the Military Wife*, a soldier's spouse is described as a woman who "must be a patriot, a helpmate, lover, comforter, and confidant to her husband . . . courageous and resilient, and have a sense of humor."

As these women wrote of their travels, many related a comedy of errors often brought on by their naivety on the trail or their ignorance of the unique situations in which they found themselves, such as trying to cook during a dust storm or chasing uninvited creatures around their rough-built homes. Who could not laugh as first-time mother Frances Boyd trustingly cut off her baby's eyelashes thinking they would grow thicker, while her husband pinched the child's nose with a clothespin believing the excruciating pain the child endured would improve her looks?

All seemed to enjoy the mirages they envisioned as they made their way across burning desert sand, admiring castles in the air and cool water holes that disappeared as they approached the dazzling, unattainable images.

They accompanied their husbands wherever they were stationed, leaving family and friends they knew they might never see again, grieving over infants who could not withstand the rigors of birth under often-unsanitary conditions with little or no medical aid, and children who succumbed to disease and disaster.

They helped dispel Victorian principles that women should not involve themselves in political and social issues, and ushered in awareness that the female intellect can and must be included in shaping events happening outside the home.

They also demanded respect from their husbands and insisted on being included in major decisions and undertakings that involved the family as well as the community. They felt equally responsible in all aspects of their lives. They had learned to accept and adapt to situations beyond their imaginations.

They endured, they flourished, they prospered, they survived.

BIBLIOGRAPHY

––––––•••––––––

Adams, Kevin. *Class and Race in the Frontier Army: Military Life in the West, 1870–1890*. Norman: University of Oklahoma Press, 2009.

Alt, Betty Sowers, and Bonnie Domrose Stone. *Campfollowing: A History of the Military Wife*. New York: Praeger Publishers, 1991.

Altshuler, Constance Wynn. *Cavalry Yellow & Infantry Blue*. Tucson: Arizona Historical Society, 1991.

––––––. *For Better or For Worse: Frontier Army Life*. Camp Verde: Camp Verde Historical Society, 1982.

––––––. *Starting with Defiance: Nineteenth Century Arizona Military Posts*. Tucson: Arizona Historical Society, 1983.

Baker, Anni P. "Daughters of Mars: Army Officers' Wives and Military Culture on the American Frontier." *The Historian* 67, no. 1 (Spring 2005): 20–42.

Barnes, Will C. *Arizona Place Names*. Tucson: University of Arizona Press, 1988.

Bates, Al. "The Days of Empire at Fort Whipple." Sharlot Hall Museum. February 26, 2000. https://archives.sharlothallmuseum.org/articles/days-past-articles/1/the-days-of-empire-at-fort-whipple.

Brandes, Ray. *Frontier Military Posts of Arizona*. Globe: Dale Stuart King, Publisher, 1960.

Butler, Anne M. "Military Myopia: Prostitution on the Frontier." *Prologue Journal* 13, no. 4 (Winter 1981): 233–250.

Butruille, Susan G. *Women's Voices from the Western Frontier*. Boise, ID: Tamarack Books, Inc., 1995.

California State Military Museum. "Fort Yuma." Updated February 8, 2016. www.militarymuseum.org/FtYuma.html.

Campbell, Robin Dell. *Mistresses of the Transient Hearth: American Army Officers' Wives and Material Culture, 1840–1880*. New York: Routledge, 2005.

Collins, Thomas P. "J. C. Worthington: Fort Whipple's Lovelorn Doctor." *Territorial Times: A Publication of the Prescott Corral of Westerners International* 2, no. 2 (May 2009): 16–23. www.prescottcorral.org/wp-content/uploads/2018/12/TerritorialTimes_V4.pdf.

Dudley, Shelly. "Stalwart Army Sweetheart." *True West Magazine*. June 10, 2013.

Eales, Anne Bruner. *Army Wives on the American Frontier: Living by the Bugles*. Boulder, CO: Johnson Books, 1996.

Fischer, Christiane, ed. *Let Them Speak for Themselves: Women in the American West 1849–1900*. Hamden, CT: Archon Books, 1977.

Greene, Duane Merritt. *Ladies and Officers of the United States Army; or, American Aristocracy. A Sketch of the Social Life and Character of the Army.* Chicago: Central Publishing Co., 1880.

Huachuca Illustrated: A Magazine of the Fort Huachuca Museum. Vols. 1–11. Sierra Vista: Fort Huachuca Historical Museum Society, 1993–1999.

Jameson, Elizabeth. "Toward a Multicultural History of Women in the Western United States." *Signs* 13, no. 4 (Summer 1988): 761–791.

Knight, Oliver. *Life and Manners in the Frontier Army.* Norman: University of Oklahoma Press, 1978.

Lahti, Janne. *Cultural Construction of an Empire.* Lincoln: University of Nebraska Press, 2012.

Langellier, John P. *Southern Arizona Military Outposts.* Charleston, SC: Arcadia Publishing, 2011.

Leckie, Shirley Anne, ed. *The Colonel's Lady on the Western Frontier: The Correspondence of Alice Kirk Grierson.* Lincoln: University of Nebraska Press, 1989.

Lockwood, Frank C. "Early Military Posts in Arizona." *Arizona Historical Review* 2, no. 4 (January 1930): 91–97.

Luchetti, Cathy. *Home on the Range: A Culinary History of the American West.* New York: Villard Books, 1993.

Mattes, Merrill J. *Indians, Infants and Infantry: Andrew and Elizabeth Burt on the Frontier.* Denver, CO: The Old West Publishing Co., 1960.

McChristian, Douglas C. *Fort Bowie, Arizona: Combat Post of the Southwest, 1858–1894.* Norman: University of Oklahoma Press, 2006.

Myres, Sandra L., ed. *Cavalry Wife: The Diary of Eveline M. Alexander, 1866–1867.* College Station: Texas A&M University Press, 1977.

———. "Romance and Reality on the American Frontier: Views of Army Wives." *Western Historical Quarterly* 13, no. 4 (October 1982): 409–427.

Nacy, Michele J. *Members of the Regiment: Army Officers' Wives on the Western Frontier, 1865–1890.* Westport, CT: Greenwood Press, 2000.

National Park Service. "19th Century Army Wives." Updated February 26, 2015. www.nps.gov/gois/learn/historyculture/army-wives.htm.

Overstreet, Daphne. *Arizona Territory Cook Book.* Phoenix: Golden West Publishers, 2004.

Roe, Frances M. A. *Army Letters from an Officer's Wife, 1871–1888.* New York: D. Appleton and Company, 1909.

Santa Fe Trail Research Site. Fort Larned Outpost: Quarterly Newsletter of Fort Larned National Historic Site and Fort Larned Old Guard. 1991–2020. www.santafetrailresearch.com/fort-larned/outpost.html.

Schaefer, Christina Kassabian. *The Hidden Half of the Family: A Sourcebook for Women's Genealogy.* Baltimore, MD: Genealogy Publishing Co., Inc., 1999.

Sibbald, John R. "Camp Followers All." *American West* 3, no. 2 (Spring 1966): 56–67.

Smith, Bill W. "Martha Dunham Summerhayes: Correcting the Biographical Record." *Journal of Arizona History* 37, mo. 1 (Spring 1996): 67–72.

Smith, Shannon D. *Give Me Eighty Men: Women and the Myth of the Fetterman Fight*. Lincoln: University of Nebraska Press, 2008.

Smith, Sherry L. *The View from Officers' Row: Army Perceptions of Western Indians*. Tucson: University of Arizona Press, 1995.

Stallard, Patricia Y., ed. *Fanny Dunbar Corbusier: Recollections of Her Army Life, 1869–1908*. Norman: University of Oklahoma Press, 2003.

——. *Glittering Misery: Dependents of the Indian Fighting Army*. Norman: University of Oklahoma Press, 1978.

Summerhayes, Martha. *Vanished Arizona*. Salem, MA: Salem Press, 1911. Reprint of the second edition. Lincoln: University of Nebraska Press, 1979.

University of Nebraska–Lincoln. "Army Officers' Wives on the Great Plains, 1865–1900." Center for Digital Research in the Humanities. n.d. plainshumanities.unl .edu/army_officers_wives/.

Wier, James A. "19th Century Army Doctors on the Frontier and in Nebraska." *Nebraska History* 61, no. 2 (Summer 1980): 192–214.

Wood, Cynthia A. "Army Laundresses and Civilization on the Western Frontier." *Journal of the West*, 42 (Summer 2002): 26–34.

——. *The Halo of Tradition: Social and Military Duty in the Frontier Army in Arizona, 1870–1890*. Publisher unknown, 1998.

Wooster, Robert. *The American Military Frontiers: The United States Army in the West, 1783–1900*. Albuquerque: University of New Mexico Press, 2009.

THE WOMEN
Mary Wildman Adams:
Adams, Mary W. "An Arizona Adventure." *The Midland Monthly* 1 (January–June 1894): 284–286.. Des Moines, IA: Johnson Brigham, Publisher.

Altshuler, Constance Wynn. *Chains of Command: Arizona and the Army, 1856–1875*. Tucson: Arizona Historical Society, 1981.

Cozzens, Peter, ed. *Eyewitness to the Indian Wars 1865–1890: The Struggle for Apacheria, Volume 1*. Mechanicsburg, PA: Stackpole Books, 2001.

"Final Respects Are Paid Mrs. J. Q. Adams." *Norwalk Reflector-Herald*. November 16, 1917.

Henry, Guy V. *Military Record of the Army and Civilian Appointments in the United States Army, Volume 1*. New York: D. Van Nostrand, 1873.

"Honored Resident Called by Death." *Norwalk Reflector-Herald*. November 12, 1917.

"Norwalk, It's Men, Women and Girls." *The Firelands Pioneer*. Norwalk, OH: Firelands Historical Society/The American Publishers Company, 1918: 2097-2098.

"Obituaries." *The Firelands Pioneer*, Vol. XXI. Norwalk, OH: Firelands Historical Society/The American Publishers Company, January 1920: 2422–2423.

Ellen McGowan Biddle:
Biddle, Ellen McGowan. *Reminiscences of a Soldier's Wife*. Philadelphia, PA: J. B. Lippincott Company, 1907.

Spence, Mary Lee, ed. *The Arizona Diary of Lily Frémont.* Tucson: University of Arizona Press, 1997.

Tefertiller, Casey. *Wyatt Earp: The Life Behind the Legend.* New York: John Wiley & Sons, Inc., 1997.

University of Nebraska–Lincoln. "Army Officers' Wives on the Great Plains, 1865–1900." Center for Digital Research in the Humanities. n.d. plainshumanities.unl .edu/army_officers_wives/.

Sarah Bowman:

Elliott, J. F. "The Great Western: Sarah Bowman, Mother and Mistress to the U.S. Army." *The Journal of Arizona History* 30, No. 1 (Spring 1989): 1–26.

Hamilton, Nancy. "The Great Western." In *The Women Who Made the West.* New York: Doubleday & Co., Inc., 1980: 186–197.

Hutton, Paul Andrew. "The Great Western." *True West Magazine.* August 22, 2017.

Moynahan, Jay. *Sarah Bowman: Pioneer Madam.* Spokane, WA: Chickadee Publishing, 2004.

Sandwich, Brian. *The Great Western: Legendary Lady of the Southwest.* El Paso: Texas Western Press, 1991.

Wettemann, Robert P., Jr. "The Girl I Left Behind Me? United States Army Laundresses and the Mexican War." *Army History,* no. 46 (Fall 1998–Winter 1999): 1–10.

Woodward, Arthur. *The Great Western: Amazon of the Army.* San Francisco, CA: Yerba Buena Chapter, National Cemetery of San Francisco, May 13, 1961.

Frances Anne Mullen Boyd:

Boyd, Mrs. Orsemus Bronson. *Cavalry Life in Tent and Field.* New York: J. Selwin Tait & Sons, 1894.

Clan Boyd Society, International. "Cavalry Life in Tent and Field." Mrs. Orsemus Bronson Boyd. 1894. homepages.rootsweb.com/~clanboyd/orsemus.htm.

James, D. Clayton. *The Years of MacArthur, 1880–1941.* Volume 1. Boston: Houghton Mifflin, 1970.

United States Congressional Series Set, Volume 2605. 50th Congress, 1st Session. House of Representatives. Report No. 2691.

Katharine Sadler Madison Cochran:

Author's interview with Julie Kettleman, great-great-great granddaughter of Katharine Cochran, November 2016.

Author's interview with Suzy Bradley, great-great granddaughter of Katharine Cochran, November 2016.

Cochran, Mrs. M. A. *Posie; or, From Reveille to Retreat. An Army Story.* Cincinnati, OH: The Robert Clarke Company, 1896.

Julia Edith Kirkham Davis:

Letters from Murray Davis to his regimental commanders requesting additional leave while in Europe, 1868–1869. fold3.com.

BIBLIOGRAPHY

"Mrs. Murry's Trip to Fort Mcdowell in 1869." Tucson: Arizona Historical Society Manuscript file. Davis, Murry (Mrs.) (Mrs. Davis is erroneously listed as Mrs. Murry.)

Schreier, Jim. "'For This I Had Left Civilization:' Julia Davis at Camp Mcdowell, 1869–1870." *Journal of Arizona History* 29, No. 2 (Summer, 1988): 185–198.

Alice Garrison Dryer:

"A Soldier Town. Fort Larned National Historic Site in Pawnee County, Kansas." HMdb.org. The Historical Marker Database. www.hmdb.org/marker .asp?marker=40157.

Dixon, Celeste. "Post Commander: Major Hiram Dryer." Santa Fe Trail Research Site. Fort Larned Outpost: Quarterly Newsletter of the Fort Larned National Historic Site and Fort Larned Old Guard. 2012. www.santafetrailresearch.com/fort -larned/outpost-v22-n4-12.html.

National Park Service. Hiram Dryer. Fort Larned National Historic Site Kansas. Updated May 21, 2019. https://www.nps.gov/fols/learn/historyculture/hiram-dryer .htm.

Sister Alice of the Community of Saint Mary (Alice Dryer). *Reminiscences of an Army Woman.* New York: United States Military Academy Library, Special Collections Division, Undated.

Alice Carey Applegate Sargent:

Burke, Arthur Meredyth, ed. *The Prominent Families of the United States of America.* London, UK: Sackfield Press, 1908.

Clark, Edward B. "Sargent, Ablest U.S. Strategist Asserts Author." *Medford Mail Tribune* (Medford, Oregon) Nov. 20, 1917. Article taken from the *Boston Transcript*, written by Edward B. Clark, on staff of *Chicago Post*.

Cullum's Register, 2991. Updated February 22, 2017. penelope.uchicago.edu/ Thayer/E/Gazetteer/Places/America/United_States/Army/USMA/Cullums_ Register/2991*.html.

"Death Claims Pioneer Woman," undated newspaper article.

Flora, Stephanie, ed. "Emigrants to Oregon in 1843." n.d.t www.oregonpioneers.com/ 1843.htm.

Kingsnorth, Carolyn. "Following the Flag. Pioneer Profiles." *Jacksonville Review*, May 2015. https://jacksonvillereview.com/following-the-flag-by-carolyn-kingsnorth/.

Sargent, Alice Applegate. "A Sketch of the Rogue River Valley and Southern Oregon History." *The Quarterly of the Oregon Historical Society* 22, no. 1 (March 1921): 1–11. (Alice read this paper before the Greater Medford Club, Spring 1915.)

Sargent, Alice Applegate. *Following the Flag: Diary of a Soldier's Wife.* Kansas City, MO: E. B. Barnett, 1909.

The Table Rock Sentinel: Newsletter of the Southern Oregon Historical Society. February 1984.

Mary Henrietta Banks Stacey:

"Gen. Sherman in Arizona." *Army and Navy Journal*. April 22, 1882.

Lesley, Lewis Burt, ed. *Uncle Sam's Camels: The Journal of May Humphreys Stacey Supplemented by the Report of Edward Fitzgerald Beale (1857-1858)*. Cambridge, MA: Harvard University Press, 1929.

Letters from Kathleen Hiatt to Miss Eleanor B. Sloan dated May 30, 1950. Tucson: Arizona Historical Society.

Myres, Sandra L., and May Banks Stacey. "An Arizona Camping Trip: May Banks Stacey's Account of an Outing to Mount Graham in 1879." *Arizona and the West* 23, no. 1 (Spring 1981): 53-64.

Rocks, David T. "Mrs. May Banks Stacey." *Theosophical History* 6, no. 4 (October 1996): 144-150.

Stacey, May Banks. Stacey Letters and Newspaper Clippings, ca. 1877-1885. Tucson: Arizona Historical Society Manuscript File No. 0757. Some of the newspaper sources cannot be identified although most of the articles were published in the *Altoona (PA) Tribune*.

Jane Earl Thorpy:

Holmes, Alice D. "'And I Was Always with Him:' The Life of Jane Thorpy, Army Laundress." Tucson: *The Journal of Arizona History* 38, no. 2 (Summer 1997): 177-190.

Lawrence, Jennifer J. *Soap Suds Row: The Bold Lives of Army Laundresses, 1802-1876*. Glendo, WY: High Plains Press, 2016.

Stewart, J. Miller. "Army Laundresses: Ladies of the 'Soap Suds Row.'" *Nebraska History* 61, no. 4 (Winter 1980): 421-436.

Sarah Elvira Camp Upham:

"Accidentally Shot Himself." *The San Francisco Call*. October 18, 1899.

Altshuler, Constance Wynn manuscript collection, FM MSS 113. Phoenix: Arizona Historical Society-Papago Park.

"Mrs. Sarah Upham Died in New York." *Dixon Evening Telegraph*. November 28, 1921.

Upham, F. Manuscript file. Tucson: Arizona Historical Society.

Upham, F. K., compiler. *Genealogy & Family History of the Uphams, of Castine, Maine and Dixon*. Newark, NJ. Advertiser Printing House. Printed for private circulation, 1887.

Upham, F. K. "Incidents of Regular Army Life in Time of Peace." *Overland Monthly* 5, Issue 28. (April-May 1885): 423-429.

U.S. Statutes at Large, Volume 31, Part 2.

INDEX

ABOUT THE AUTHOR

Chris Richard Photography, Tucson, Arizona

Jan Cleere has been writing about the people of the desert southwest for over twenty years. Her books include the award-winning TwoDot publications *"Never Don't Pay Attention:" The Life of Rodeo Photographer Louise L. Serpa* (New Mexico/Arizona Book Award for best Arizona biography), *Outlaw Tales of Arizona* (National Federation of Press Women Award for best nonfiction), *Amazing Girls of Arizona: True Stories of Young Pioneers* (Arizona Book Publishers Glyph Award for best juvenile/young adult nonfiction), and *Nevada's Remarkable Women* (Women Writing the West WILLA Award finalist in nonfiction). She also writes a monthly column for Tucson's *Arizona Daily Star* newspaper, "Western Women," detailing the lives of early Arizona pioneers. Her freelance work appears in national and regional publications.